I0427257

NEXT LEVEL

SELLING

NEXT LEVEL

LIFE

THE COMPLETE GUIDE TO SELLING

MICHAEL PAULK

Copyright © 2022 by Michael Paulk. All rights reserved.

The work contained herein has been produced with the intent to provide relevant knowledge and information on the topic described in the title for entertainment purposes only. While the author has gone to every extent to furnish up-to-date and accurate information, no claims can be made as to its accuracy or validity as the author has made no claims to be an expert. on this topic. Notwithstanding, the reader is asked to do their own research and consult any subject matter experts they deem necessary to ensure the quality and accuracy of the material presented herein.

This statement is legally binding as deemed by the Committee of Publishers Association and the American Bar Association for the territory of the United States. Other jurisdictions may apply their own legal statutes—any reproduction, transmission, or copying of this material contained in this work without the copyright holder's express written consent shall be deemed a copyright violation as per the current legislation in force on the date of publishing and subsequent time thereafter. This copyright holder may claim all additional works derived from this material.

The data, depictions, events, descriptions, and all other information forthwith are considered to be true, fair, and accurate unless the work is expressly described as a work of fiction. Regardless of the nature of this work, the Publisher is exempt from any responsibility for actions taken by the reader in conjunction with this work. The Publisher acknowledges that the reader acts of their own accord and releases the author and Publisher of any responsibility for observing tips, advice, counsel, strategies, and techniques that may be offered in this volume.

Contents

INTRODUCTION

Imagine a world where the word "selling" isn't synonymous with pushing, persuading, or pestering. Picture yourself seamlessly guiding a conversation that ends not with a pressured "yes" but with an enthusiastic "let's do this!" from your prospect. This is not a distant utopia; it's the reality I will guide you to in "Next Level Selling - Next Level Life." Dive into the heart of consultative selling, a strategy where understanding eclipses ultimatums. Unlock the power of genuine connections, craft questions that uncover true needs, and tailor your approach to resonate deeply with each unique individual you encounter. Forget the archaic closing techniques that feel like a battle; I'll show you how to make sales feel like an alliance. Lesson number one? Never embattle your prospect. So, why should you trust me? My journey from the disciplined ranks of the U.S. Army's 82d Airborne Division, the 75th Ranger Regiment, and 1st SFOD-D to the competitive world of finance, owning a boxing gym and the auto industry has forged a sales philosophy that's tested, triumphant, and transformative. Have you ever wondered what it feels like to sell without selling? To have clients eager to proceed because you've touched a chord, not because they've been cornered. Stay with me. By the last page, you'll have learned to elevate your sales game and live a next-level life. But first, let's address the question you might be asking: How can a conversation be your most powerful selling tool? The answer lies just ahead at the crest of this uncharted territory. And believe me, you'll want to see what's on the other side.

Imagine stepping into a world where every interaction you have isn't just a transaction but a step towards a meaningful connection, where the art of selling transcends the mere exchange of goods for money and becomes a symphony of shared understanding and mutual gain. This is not merely a vision; it's a tangible reality that awaits you within these pages. You are about to embark on a journey that will revolutionize how you sell and transform how you perceive every aspect of your life. Welcome to "Next Level Selling - Next Level Life."

As you traverse the landscape of this book, you will uncover the secrets of consultative selling. This paradigm-shifting approach prizes the discovery of your customer's needs above all else. You will learn to build relationships based on trust, empathy, and insight. I promise you this: By embracing the principles laid out in this book, you will achieve greater sales success and experience a profound shift in your personal and professional life.

But why should you believe such a bold assertion? Because the methods I'm about to share are not just untested theories but are forged from real-world experience. From the discipline of my 15 years of military service in some of the most elite units of the U.S. Army to the cutthroat arenas of finance and the auto industry, I have honed a set of skills that have consistently proven their worth. I have distilled these lessons into a set of strategies that are as effective as they are transformative.

Now, I know what you might be thinking. The sales world has books that make grandiose promises only to rehash the same tired tactics. You may be skeptical, and rightly so. But let me reassure you that "Next Level Selling - Next Level Life" differs. The techniques within these pages are not about manipulation or high- pressure tactics. Instead, they focus on the power of great communication, the ability to ask the right questions, and truly listen to the answers. I'll show you that the best salespeople don't close; they open a dialogue, a partnership, and a path to mutual success.

Envision yourself at the end of this journey. You've turned pages filled with insights and exercises and implemented strategies that felt like they were written just for you. The transformation is palpable. You no longer chase clients; they come to you, drawn by the reputation you've built as someone who understands, cares, and delivers solutions that resonate on a personal level. Your sales numbers have soared, not because you've pushed harder but because you've connected deeper. And it's not just your professional life that's seen a change. The skills you've learned have seeped into every interaction, every relationship, and every moment of your day-to-day life, elevating it to the next level.

This is the commitment I ask of you: to read this book and engage with it actively. To challenge yourself to apply its principles and reap the rewards of true selling mastery. You are not simply holding a book; you are holding a new way of life.

So, let's begin. Let's unravel the tapestry of traditional selling and reweave it into something far more vibrant and fulfilling. Let's dive into the heart of what it means to connect, to understand, and to succeed. Let's take the first step into a grander world where selling is not a task but a journey, not a job but a joy.

Welcome to "Next Level Selling - Next Level Life." Let's do this!

CHAPTER 1

THE SALES MINDSET: EMBRACING THE CONSULTANT WITHIN

The Psychology of Sales Success

In pursuing sales excellence, one cannot overlook the profound role psychology plays in shaping a salesperson's success. It's an intricate dance of the mind where strategy, empathy, and self- awareness converge to create an environment where transactions flourish and relationships grow. But what mental attributes and habits set apart successful salespeople? How do they develop these qualities? And perhaps most importantly, how can you cultivate these traits to enhance your sales performance and elevate your life to the next level?

A fundamental truth lies at the core of every sales interaction: we are not merely exchanging products or services but engaging in complex human interaction. The best salespeople understand this.

They know that beneath the surface of every conversation are layers of emotion, motivation, and desire. They rely on a keen understanding of human psychology to tap into these layers—not as a manipulation tool but as a bridge to genuine connection.

The claim at the heart of this chapter is simple yet profound: a salesperson's mindset is as crucial to their success as their sales skills. Mental resilience, emotional intelligence, and an unshakable belief in the value of their offering are the hallmarks of those who achieve their quotas and redefine them.

Consider the primary evidence supporting this claim: a study by the Sales Management Association reveals that sales professionals with high emotional intelligence (EQ) outperform their lower-EQ counterparts by a significant margin. Emotional intelligence—the ability to perceive, control, and evaluate emotions—allows top salespeople to read the room, build rapport, and respond to clients' needs in real-time.

Diving deeper into this evidence, we see that emotional intelligence is not a fixed attribute but a set of skills that can be developed and refined. Salespeople with high EQ are adept at self-regulation, allowing them to remain composed in the face of rejection or stress. They exhibit a high level of empathy, enabling them to understand and address the emotional drivers behind their clients' decisions. Moreover, they possess superb social skills, facilitating powerful networking and building long-term relationships.

Yet, as persuasive as this evidence may be, one must also consider counterarguments. Skeptics might point to the countless daily sales without any apparent need for a deep emotional connection. They might argue that a strong product, competitive pricing, and an aggressive sales strategy are sufficient for success.

In response, it is essential to clarify that while these factors are undoubtedly important, they represent only a fraction of the sales equation. The rebuttal to this counterargument lies in the countless testimonials of customers who chose a particular product or service because of the salesperson. People buy from people, and a salesperson's connection with their client can be the deciding factor when all other variables are equal.

To bolster this point, let's bring in additional supporting evidence. Research by Gallup has shown that companies with engaged employees—those who are deeply involved in and enthusiastic about their work—outperform their competitors by 147% in earnings per share. Engagement is not a matter of mere job satisfaction; it reflects the passion and commitment that employees, particularly salespeople, bring to their roles. It underscores the importance of a mindset focused on building genuine connections and delivering exceptional value.

As we conclude this exploration, the reinforced assertion stands clear and compelling: the psychology of a salesperson is a critical determinant of their success. It's not merely about techniques and tactics; it's about cultivating a mindset that values relationships, understands the human element in every sale, and recognizes the importance of emotional intelligence in forging lasting connections.

So, as you turn the page, ask yourself: are you ready to delve into the depths of your psychology? Are you prepared to embrace the mental habits that can elevate your sales numbers and every facet of your life? The journey ahead is challenging, but the rewards are limitless for those willing to engage with it wholeheartedly.

Remember, in sales, as in life, the mind is the battlefield, and victory belongs to skilled and psychologically attuned people. Let's continue to unravel the secrets of this inner game, for it is here, in the realm of the mind, that true sales mastery awaits.

Curiosity as a Sales Virtue

A particular trait quietly asserts its significance, often overlooked amidst the more blatant qualities like assertiveness and persuasiveness. This trait is curiosity. It might seem quaint, almost too simple, but its impact on the sales process and the resulting relationship with the customer is anything but trivial.

Curiosity, in its essence, is the desire to learn or know more about something or someone. It is a driving force that propels salespeople to move beyond superficial interactions and delve into the heart of their customers' needs, wants, and situations. By fostering genuine curiosity, a salesperson can uncover valuable insights that can guide the sales process to a successful resolution that benefits both the seller and the buyer.

When we elaborate on the key elements of curiosity, we see it encompasses an eagerness to explore, a willingness to ask questions and an openness to new experiences. A curious salesperson is someone who does not assume to know what the customer wants but is eager to find out by asking open-ended questions and listening intently to the answers.

Curiosity has driven human progress; it's why we've explored unknown lands and reached for the stars. It's a fundamental aspect of our nature embedded within our very DNA. In the context of sales, this innate drive can be harnessed to foster deeper understanding and create stronger connections with clients.

Placed within a broader framework, curiosity is a component of emotional intelligence. It is linked to empathy, another critical sales virtue, as both require an awareness of others' perspectives and experiences. When combined, these traits create a potent mix that can lead to more meaningful interactions and, ultimately, more successful sales endeavors.

Real-world applications of curiosity in sales are numerous. Imagine a salesperson who starts by asking the customer about their day-to-day challenges instead of launching into a pitch. Through this dialogue, the salesperson might discover that the customer has unmet needs, which can be addressed by the product or service being sold.

A common misconception about curiosity is that it's an innate talent—you either have it or you don't. However, like many aspects of emotional intelligence, curiosity can be cultivated and refined. It can be encouraged through active listening, asking better questions, and maintaining an open mind.

But let us delve deeper still. Why should we value curiosity so highly in the context of sales? Because it conveys respect and genuine interest in the customer, transforming the dynamic from a transactional exchange to a consultative partnership. A curious salesperson learns to read between the lines of what is said and what is left unsaid, identifying opportunities and pain points that may not be immediately apparent.

Let's paint a scenario: a customer, weary from interactions with salespeople who seem only to push their agenda, encounters a salesperson who asks, "What's the biggest challenge you're facing right now?" This simple inquiry, driven by curiosity, can open doors to a dialogue that feels less like a sales pitch and more like a problem-solving session.

And so, we must ask ourselves, how often do we approach our customers with genuine curiosity? Have we taken the time to understand their businesses and their personal goals and challenges? Are we truly listening or just waiting for our turn to speak?

Let's be direct in reducing the use of adjectives and adverbs: curiosity matters. It is the unseen muscle that, when flexed, can elevate our sales approach from mundane to remarkable. It allows us to craft solutions that resonate on a personal level with our customers, and in doing so, we don't just sell; we build relationships that endure.

To further emphasize, consider this single-line paragraph: Curiosity is the gateway to customer-centric selling. Always remember this: when we approach our clients with a curious mind, we do more than sell; we engage in a collaborative journey of discovery. We foster trust, we create value, and we set the stage for a next-level life not just for ourselves but for everyone we do business with. Curiosity is not just a sales virtue; it's a life virtue. So, let us step forward with inquisitive minds, for it is through curiosity that we unlock the true potential of our sales careers and our lives.

Trust-Building Techniques

When it comes to sales, a currency is more valuable than the figures on an invoice: the trust between a salesperson and their client. Pursuing trust is akin to threading a needle—demanding finesse, patience, and a steady hand. Master this, and you've unlocked the door to immediate sales and the gateway to enduring client relationships and a fulfilling life, both professionally and personally.

Your objective, then, is not merely to implement trust-building strategies but to weave them into the very fabric of your sales approach, ensuring that every interaction with a client lays another brick in the foundation of a solid, trusting relationship.

Before embarking on this journey, let's gather the necessary materials or prerequisites. You'll need a genuine interest in your clients, an ability to listen actively, a commitment to transparency, and a dedication to fulfilling promises. Moreover, possessing knowledge about your products or services, understanding the industry, and having the right tools to manage client relationships are instrumental.

Let's begin with a broad overview. The trust-building process encompasses several phases: rapport building, needs analysis, solution offering, handling objections, closing, and post-sale service. Each step requires specific actions do strengthen the client's trust in you.

As we dive into detailed steps, remember the first encounter sets the tone. Start by establishing rapport with a warm greeting, a smile, and a genuine interest in knowing your client. Ask about their business, their challenges, and their aspirations. Listen more than you speak, and when you do talk, ensure it's to echo their concerns, validate their feelings, or offer insights that resonate with their situation.

Conduct a thorough needs analysis by asking open-ended questions and encouraging clients to express themselves freely. This demonstrates that you value their input and provides invaluable information to tailor your solutions.

When offering solutions, do so with the client's best interest. Exhibit how your product or service aligns with their needs. Be transparent about what your offering can and cannot do, avoiding over-promising and under-delivering.

Handling objections is an art form. View each objection as an opportunity to deepen your understanding of the client's concerns. Respond with empathy, provide clarifications, and, if possible, adjust your offering to suit their needs better.

The closing phase should feel natural, a mutual agreement that your solution is the right choice. Ensure all terms are clear and no lingering doubts or unanswered questions exist.

After the sale, continue to provide excellent service. Check-in with your client to ensure they're satisfied and address any issues promptly. This shows you care about the long-term success of their business, not just the sale.

Now, let's offer some tips and warnings. Always be honest, even if it means admitting a mistake—this can strengthen trust. Remember that trust is easily broken and hard to rebuild, so avoid making commitments you can't keep. And always maintain professionalism; your reliability is a testament to your character.

To test or validate trust, solicit feedback from your clients. Are they comfortable sharing information with you? Do they seek your advice? Positive responses to these questions are good indicators that trust has been established.

If you sense a client's trust waning in troubleshooting, address it head-on. Ask for their candid feedback, and be prepared to change your approach if necessary.

Let me paint you a picture. Imagine a client's sigh of relief when they realize you're not just another salesperson but a trusted advisor with their best interests at heart. That sense of comfort is the reward of trust-building.

What's the biggest obstacle you face in establishing trust? Reflect on this, for it's often the hurdles we're most reluctant to address that, once overcome, lead to the most significant growth.

In the spirit of using simple language, let's be clear: building trust is both an art and a science. It demands of us not just skill but heart.

Consider this one-line paragraph for emphasis: Trust is the bedrock of lasting relationships.

By now, you should feel the rhythm of our conversation, the ebb and flow of ideas as we explore the nuances of trust in sales.

As we conclude, remember the words of Stephen R. Covey: "Trust is the glue of life. It's the most essential ingredient in effective communication. It's the foundational principle that holds all relationships." So, in your subsequent encounter, whether it's with a new lead or a long-standing client, pause and ask yourself, "How can I build trust here?"

Let these strategies become second nature, let them guide you, and watch as your sales and your life ascend to the next level.

Active Listening in Sales

The power of hearing is often overshadowed by the urgency to speak. Yet, the most successful sales professionals find their edge in quiet listening. Active listening is not merely a passive process but a strategic tool that can unlock deeper customer insights, foster meaningful connections, and drive sales to new heights.

Imagine conversing with a potential client, armed not with a catalog of rehearsed pitches but with an attentive ear and a keen understanding. This scenario epitomizes the essence of active listening in sales—a skill that transforms ordinary interactions into opportunities for growth and connection.

The Concept:

Active listening involves fully concentrating, understanding, responding, and remembering what is said in a conversation. It's about being present in the moment and engaging with the speaker verbally and nonverbally. This means nodding in agreement, maintaining eye contact, and offering verbal affirmations like "I see" or "That makes sense." More than just a courteous nod, active listening enables you to read between the lines to grasp the words, emotions, and intentions behind them.

Some Examples and Illustrations:

Consider Sarah, a sales associate who met with a long-time client, Mr. Thompson. Instead of launching into a pitch for the latest product, Sarah asked open-ended questions and listened. She noticed a hint of frustration in Mr. Thompson's voice as he discussed his team's challenges. By probing gently and listening actively, Sarah uncovered concerns that no product brochure could address. Her solution was tailored to Mr. Thompson's unique situation, which led to a sale and strengthened their professional relationship.

There are Different Perspectives:

Active listening is not without its critics. Some argue that there isn't always time to listen at length in fast-paced sales environments. However, the value of understanding your customers' needs and pain points can significantly outweigh the time invested. Others worry about over-empathizing and losing sight of the sales goal. Yet, those who master active listening know it is about balance— aligning customer needs with business objectives.

Some Data and Facts:

Research supports the practice of active listening. A study by the International Listening Association found that listening can influence up to 40% of a salesperson's job performance. Moreover, a Salesforce survey revealed that customers who feel understood are 4.6 times more likely to feel empowered and trust a business.

Hearing Versus Listening:

Active listening is often confused with similar terms, such as 'hearing.' Hearing is a physiological process, while active listening is a psychological one that requires conscious effort. Empathy, another term frequently mentioned alongside active listening, is the ability to understand and share the feelings of another. Active listening is a pathway to heart, allowing a salesperson to connect with their customer on a deeper level.

A Few Key Takeaways:

To encapsulate the discussion, remember that active listening is a multifaceted tool in sales. It allows you to understand your customers beyond surface-level interactions, creating solutions that resonate on a personal level. Active listening builds trust, fosters loyalty, and can set you apart in a crowded marketplace. By integrating this skill into your sales approach, you not only elevate your professional practice but also enhance the quality of your interactions, leading to a more prosperous and fulfilling life.

As you progress in your sales journey, carry with you the understanding that every conversation is an opportunity to listen, learn, and connect. Let the art of active listening be the compass that guides you to the next level.

Resilience and Rejection Handling

The harsh sting of rejection is an all-too-familiar sensation. It's an experience that can either forge the steel of resilience within a salesperson or erode their confidence bit by bit. Yet, the ability to confront and utilize rejection is not just a skill—it's an art that, when mastered, can elevate one's approach to sales and life itself.

Picture this scenario: You've just delivered a pitch that you believe is flawless. The product is perfect, the timing impeccable, and your presentation is spot on. But despite your best efforts, the answer is a resounding "no." You're left questioning your approach, your product, and perhaps even your career choice. It's a crossroads moment that every salesperson faces.

The problem, as stark as it is, is not the rejection itself but how it is processed and internalized. If left unchecked, the fear of rejection can be debilitating, leading to a downward spiral of self-doubt and missed opportunities. The consequences of not addressing this issue are significant – reduced job performance, lower job satisfaction, and a potentially high turnover rate within sales teams.

But there is a silver lining, a solution that can turn the tide. The key lies in developing resilience, enabling individuals to bounce back from setbacks stronger. Strength in sales means viewing rejection not as a personal failure but as a valuable learning experience—an integral part of the journey toward success. The main point of my first book, "Always bite off more than you can chew," is based on this concept: being resilient!

To cultivate this resilience, begin by redefining your relationship with rejection. Adopt a growth mindset where each "no" brings you closer to a "yes." Instead of dwelling on the negative, dissect the experience. What can be learned? Was there a mismatch in customer needs and product offerings? Could the pitch be refined? This analytical approach takes the sting out of rejection and replaces it with strategic improvement.

Implementing this mindset requires a series of actionable steps. First, set realistic goals and expectations for each interaction. Celebrate the small wins, like a client taking the time to listen to your pitch, even if they don't make a purchase. Second, develop a support network of colleagues and mentors who can provide constructive feedback and encouragement. Third, practice self-care and stress-reduction techniques to maintain mental and emotional well-being.

Evidence of the effectiveness of this solution abounds. Sales professionals who embrace rejection as part of their growth process often report increased motivation and better sales outcomes. A study published in the Journal of Personality and Social Psychology found that individuals who viewed failure as a learning opportunity were more likely to experience subsequent success.

While building resilience is the primary solution, alternative strategies exist to handle rejection. One such system is to diversify one's approach to sales, not relying too heavily on any single method or client. Another is to enhance one's sales skills through continuous training and education, thereby reducing the likelihood of rejection.

Have you ever wondered why some salespeople handle rejection with grace while others crumble? The answer lies within the fabric of their mindset and their preparedness to turn setbacks into stepping stones. By nurturing resilience, we fortify our professional endeavors and enrich our personal lives. Rejection, when navigated adroitly, becomes not a roadblock but a stepping stone to greater achievement and fulfillment.

Let's pause for a moment. Take a deep breath and reflect on your sales experiences. Can you recall a time when rejection led to introspection, learning, and growth? It is these moments that shape the contours of a successful sales career.

In conclusion, the sales journey is as much about personal development as it is about revenue. It's a path strewn with the rocks of rejection, but by walking it with resilience, we can transform those rocks into milestones. As we continue to explore the principles of 'Next Level Selling - Next Level Life,' remember that each rejection is an invitation to rise, refine, and redefine the art of selling. Embrace, learn from, and let it propel you to levels of success and satisfaction you never imagined possible.

The Consultative Salesperson's Toolkit

Transitioning from a traditional approach to a consultative one can be transformative. The consultative salesperson's toolkit is not just a set of techniques; it's a paradigm shift that places the client's needs at the forefront of every interaction. This approach fosters a collaborative partnership between salesperson and client, leading to solutions that resonate on a deeper level and, ultimately, to a more fulfilling life for the sales professional who practices it.

Before we dive into the intricacies of the consultative salesperson's toolkit, let's understand why it's crucial to the modern sales landscape. In a market saturated with products and services, the differentiator is no longer just the quality or the price—it's the experience and the value that a salesperson brings to the table. Adopting a consultative demeanor sets the stage for a relationship built on trust, respect, and mutual success.

Now, let's preview the core components:

1. Active Listening
2. Solution-Centric Mindset
3. Knowledge and Expertise
4. Tailored Communication
5. Relationship Building
6. Strategic Questioning
7. Value Proposition

Each element is a cog in the well-oiled machine of consultative selling. As we dissect each one, remember that it's not just about understanding the concept but mastering its application.

To truly comprehend the needs and challenges of your client, you must become an adept, active listener. This involves more than just hearing the words spoken; it's about perceiving the underlying emotions, concerns, and aspirations. An active listener pays attention to the nuances of the conversation, including tone and body language, and responds in a way that demonstrates genuine understanding.

Studies have shown that salespeople who excel at active listening are more likely to effectively identify and address client pain points. For example, a Harvard Business Review article highlighted that customers feel more valued and are more willing to engage in business when salespeople actively listen to them.

In practice, this means when a client expresses concerns about a product's integration with their existing systems, an active listener will acknowledge the issue, summarize what they've heard to confirm understanding and offer insights or solutions addressing the specific concern.

The essence of consultative selling is the relentless pursuit of the best solution for the client. This mindset shifts the focus from making a quick sale to creating long-term value. It's about understanding that success in sales is not measured by the number of deals closed but by the satisfaction and loyalty of your clients.

Evidence of the solution-centric mindset's effectiveness is abundant. A case study from the Journal of Marketing found that solution-oriented salespeople achieved higher customer satisfaction scores and repeat business rates.

Practically, this means you don't push a one-size-fits-all product when encountering a client with a unique set of challenges. Instead, you analyze their situation and propose a customized solution aligning with their goals.

To be a true consultant, you must possess an in-depth knowledge of your industry, products, and the market forces at play. This expertise enables you to provide valuable insights and recommendations that your clients might not find elsewhere.

Real-world success stories abound of sales professionals who leverage their knowledge to win trust and business. For instance, a salesperson with a deep understanding of regulatory changes was able to guide clients through a complex compliance landscape, resulting in increased client reliance and sales growth.

This expertise is not static; it requires a commitment to continuous learning and staying abreast of industry trends and changes. It's about being the go-to person for your clients when they need guidance.

Every client is unique, with distinct communication preferences and decision-making processes. A consultative salesperson can tailor their communication style to match the client's. This might mean using more data and analytics with a detail-oriented client or adopting a more narrative style for a client who values stories and examples.

A Journal of Personal Selling & Sales Management study emphasized that sales outcomes improve when communication is adapted to the buyer's style.

Practically, it's about creating a pitch that resonates with the client on a personal level. If a client values brevity and clarity, your communication should be concise and to the point, cutting through the clutter to deliver value.

The relationship between the salesperson and the client is at the heart of consultative selling. This bond is not transactional but transformational, built on trust, mutual respect, and the shared goal of achieving the client's objectives.

A Forbes article underscored the importance of relationship-building, citing that strong relationships lead to repeat business and referrals, which are crucial for long-term success.

In practice, relationship building can take many forms, from remembering personal details about your clients and checking in on them regularly to providing unsolicited value, such as relevant industry news or introductions to valuable contacts.

Asking the right questions at the right time is a powerful tool in the consultative salesperson's arsenal. It allows you to uncover the client's needs, priorities, and decision-making criteria. Strategic questioning goes beyond the superficial to reveal the core of what the client seeks to achieve.

Research supports the impact of strategic questioning, with a study from the American Psychological Association showing that well-crafted questions lead to more meaningful conversations and better outcomes.

In practice, this means asking about the client's budget or timeline and exploring their vision for the future, the challenges they face, and the impact they wish to have.

Your value proposition is the clear statement of the tangible results a client will receive from using your products or services. It's not just a list of features; it's a compelling narrative that connects those features to the client's aspirations and pain points.

A McKinsey report highlighted that a strong value proposition could be a significant differentiator, particularly in competitive markets.

This means crafting a value proposition that speaks directly to the client's situation. If a client wants to expand their business, your value proposition should articulate how your product or service will facilitate that growth.

As we weave through these elements, consider how each one applies to your sales approach. Have you truly listened to your clients or waited for your turn to speak? Are you solving their problems or your own sales targets? Reflect upon these questions as you continue to evolve in your role as a consultative salesperson.

Next Level Selling isn't just a methodology; it's a commitment to a higher standard of service and a more meaningful life in sales. By embracing the tools and techniques outlined in the consultative salesperson's toolkit, you're enhancing your professional aptitude, enriching your clients' lives, and setting the stage for unparalleled personal and professional growth.

Sales Mindset Case Studies

A particularly challenging sales scenario was unfolding in the heart of Silicon Valley, where innovation meets ambition on every street corner. Marcus, a seasoned sales representative for a cutting-edge cybersecurity firm, faced a formidable task. His prospect, a major financial institution, was grappling with increasingly sophisticated cyber threats and desperately needed a robust security solution.

Marcus, who prided himself on his consultative approach, was no ordinary salesperson. His IT security background and exceptional interpersonal skills made him a trusted advisor in the eyes of his clients. He epitomized what modern sales professionals aspire to be—a blend of expertise, empathy, and strategic acumen.

The financial institution's primary challenge was clear: they needed a cybersecurity system that was both impenetrable and compliant with the latest financial regulations. Any breach could spell disaster financially and in terms of customer trust and brand reputation.

Marcus embarked on a deep dive into the client's current security infrastructure, meticulously analyzing the gaps and vulnerabilities. His approach was not to sell but to solve. He knew understanding the client's unique environment, and pressures was paramount to tailoring a solution that would suffice and excel.

Marcus crafted a solution that seamlessly integrated with the institution's existing systems by employing his profound knowledge of cybersecurity trends and regulatory requirements. He focused on ease of implementation and scalability, ensuring the solution could adapt to evolving threats and business growth.

The results spoke volumes. The financial institution saw a significant reduction in attempted breaches and, more importantly, an enhanced sense of security among its customers. The sales figures were impressive, but for Marcus, the true reward was the strengthened relationship and the peace of mind he had provided to his client.

Reflecting on the case, it was apparent that Marcus's success hinged on several factors. His active listening skills allowed him to grasp the client's concerns genuinely. His solution-centric mindset steered the conversation from a transactional sale to a strategic partnership. His knowledge and expertise had instilled confidence, his tailored communication had resonated with the decision- makers, and his strategic questioning had uncovered deeper insights into the client's needs.

While the case study lacked visual aids, the narrative painted a vivid picture of the consultative sales process. It was a testament to the power of a sales approach, prioritizing the client's needs above all else.

This story, while unique, was not an isolated incident. It reflected a broader narrative within the sales industry—a shift towards a more client-centric, consultative approach. It underscored the importance of building genuine relationships, understanding the client's world, and delivering solutions that resonated on a deeper level.

As you ponder Marcus's story, consider this: How often do you approach a sales opportunity as a partnership rather than a transaction? Do you seek to understand before being understood? These are the questions that, when answered honestly, can propel you to the next level in selling and, by extension, in life.

Remember, the essence of Next Level Selling is not about the art of the deal but the art of the difference you make in your client's world. It's about transcending the traditional seller-buyer dynamic and fostering a relationship where both parties emerge stronger, wiser, and more successful.

As we close this chapter on Marcus's triumph, let it ignite a spark within you to pursue excellence in your sales endeavors. Embrace the lessons learned, apply them to your strategies, and watch your sales and life reach heights you never thought possible. With each client interaction, ask yourself: Am I merely selling a product, or am I enriching a life?

The next chapter will explore another real-world scenario where a consultative sales approach turned a potential loss into a ground-breaking win. Stay tuned to uncover how a deep understanding of a client's unspoken desires can unlock opportunities that lie well beyond the surface.

CHAPTER 2

THE DISCIPLINE OF SELLING

Crafting Your Daily Sales Ritual

In the competitive dance of sales, each step, each pivot, and each gesture contributes to the art of closing deals and cultivating success. But what truly sets apart the exceptional from the average is not the grandiose performances on the sales stage—it's the meticulous rehearsals behind the scenes. It's the daily sales ritual that primes you for success.

The goal here is crystalline: to construct a daily routine that conditions your mind hones your skills, and aligns your actions with sales triumph. Like a maestro leading an orchestra, you will orchestrate your day to crescendo into peak performance.

Before the symphony can begin, there are instruments to tune and scores to study. The prerequisites for this ritual are commitment, discipline, and a readiness to embrace change. You will need a planner or digital calendar, customer relationship management (CRM) system access, and an open space for morning physical and mental activation exercises.

Picture a mosaic, each tile a task, each hue a habit. Together, they form the broad overview of your daily sales ritual: morning preparation, strategic planning, customer engagement, skill development, and reflective closeout. This is the framework upon which your sales masterpiece will be painted, day after day.

Now, let us dive into each tile's intricacies and hue.

Morning preparation begins with the birth of daybreak. Awaken your body with a sequence of stretches or a brisk walk. Feel the energy coursing through your veins as you prime your physical vessel for the day's challenges. Nourish your mind with affirmations that reinforce your sales goals and intentions.

Strategic planning is the compass that guides your ship through the tumultuous sales seas. Scrutinize your CRM data, identify priority leads, and carve out specific times for outreach. Intersperse these with blocks for administrative tasks, ensuring that the minutiae do not derail your main mission.

Customer engagement is the heart of your sales ritual. It's the dialogue, the connection, the rapport. Reach out purposefully, listen intently, and contribute value in every interaction. Remember, every touchpoint is an opportunity to strengthen relationships and build trust.

Skill development is the sharpening of your sword, the refinement of your craft. Dedicate time to absorbing new sales strategies, analyzing past interactions for improvement, and role-playing scenarios with peers or mentors. Cultivate curiosity and strive for continuous learning.

Reflective closeout is the quiet after the applause, the moment to reflect on the day's performance. Assess what worked well and what missteps occurred. Jot down these insights in your journal as a lodestar for tomorrow's ritual.

Here's a little bit of advice: infuse flexibility into your routine. While structure is key, rigidity can stifle. Adapt to the unexpected with grace. And a word of caution: beware of burnout. Balance intensity with intervals of rest and recreation.

How will you know your ritual is effective? Your sales numbers will tell a story of growth, your interactions will deepen in quality, and your confidence will soar to new heights. These are the tangible and intangible metrics of success.

Should challenges arise, as they inevitably will, troubleshoot with tenacity. If mornings feel rushed, prepare the night before. When distractions abound, seek solace in time-blocking techniques. If motivation wanes, reconnect with your 'why'—the reason you embarked on this journey.

A powerful daily ritual is not crafted overnight. It results from persistence, trial and error, and commitment to excellence. As you embark on this journey, remember that every day is a fresh canvas, a new opportunity to sculpt your sales destiny.

So, are you ready to elevate your game, to move in harmony with the rhythm of success? The stage is set, and the audience awaits. It's time to perform your daily sales ritual and live your next- level life.

Long-Term Vision In Sales

As we step beyond the immediacies of daily routines and rituals, we step into a terrain that demands foresight and a panoramic view of our professional endeavors. It's the strategic realm of long-term vision in sales—a landscape that, while often overlooked in the hustle of immediate targets, holds the key to surviving and thriving in the ever-evolving marketplace.

In the sometimes-crazy sales world, where short-term gains often overshadow the horizon beyond, a pernicious issue brews. It is the myopic focus on quick wins and instant gratifications—a mindset that, while rewarding at the moment, can lead to a perilous path of missed opportunities and strategic blunders. The siren song of immediate success tempts many, but those who resist and peer into the future stand to reap the bounties of sustained growth and enduring success.

Consider the tale of two salespeople: one who chases quick deals, ignoring the seeds of future relationships, and another who nurtures prospects, investing time in understanding their evolving needs. The former may revel in short-lived victories, but the latter cultivates a garden of loyal clientele, yielding a harvest that sustains through seasons of change.

The consequences of neglecting a long-term vision can be dire. Without it, careers plateau, businesses stagnate, and once-vibrant markets wither into obsolescence. A salesperson tethered to the present is like a ship adrift without a compass—vulnerable to the capricious winds of market shifts and consumer trends. But fear not, for this is not a predestined fate. We can chart a course toward a future brimming with potential with intention and strategy.

We propose a holistic solution to remedy this oversight: developing a long-term strategic sales plan. This blueprint serves as a guiding star, ensuring that each decision, each interaction, and each sale is a deliberate step toward a grander objective. It is not merely a document but a philosophy—a commitment to the future that influences today's actions.

Implementing this vision begins with a simple yet profound shift in perspective. One must elevate from the minutiae of transactions to the grandeur of transformations. Where do you see your sales career or business in the next five, ten, or twenty years? What legacy do you aspire to leave in your industry? The answers to these questions will serve as the foundation for your long-term strategy.

Next, it's imperative to cultivate an intimate understanding of your market and customers. What are their aspirations? How are their needs evolving? How can you grow alongside them, adapting your offerings to the changing tides? This knowledge becomes the bedrock of your strategy, informing the initiatives you undertake and the relationships you foster.

Once the groundwork is laid, the strategy must translate into tangible actions. This involves setting specific, measurable goals that align with your vision. It requires the discipline to invest in relationships that may not bear fruit immediately but promise a bountiful future. It demands the courage to innovate, to venture beyond the comfort of the familiar, and to explore uncharted territories where new opportunities await.

But how do we know this approach bears fruit? History and foresight converge to answer this query. Industries are replete with stories of businesses that soared on the wings of long-term vision— those that anticipated trends, built on customer loyalty, and invested in sustainable practices. Their success stories are not mere anecdotes but a testament to the efficacy of foresight in sales.

Are there alternative solutions? Certainly, diversifying portfolios, expanding into new markets, or even restructuring sales models are all viable strategies. Each has its merits and may complement a long-term vision. However, without the underpinning of a forward-thinking plan, these efforts risk being disjointed or short-lived.

Imagine a sales career where each day's efforts are a brushstroke in a grand masterpiece—a career that transcends the transactional and becomes transformational. By embracing a long-term vision, you secure your place in the annals of sales success and elevate your life to new heights. Your professional journey becomes a narrative of growth, your legacy a tale of foresight and fortitude.

So, as you stand at this junction, with the canvas of your career unfurled before you, what strokes will you paint? Will the shiny allure of immediate gain sway you, or will you wield the brush with the poise of a visionary, crafting a legacy that endures? The choice is yours, and the time to decide is now. Will you ascend to the next level of selling and elevate your life to its next grand chapter?

Goal Setting and Achievement

Embarking on a journey of sales excellence requires more than just a penchant for persuasion and a knack for negotiation. It demands a meticulous blend of ambition and methodical planning. To transform your sales career into a relentless engine of success, you must master the art of goal-setting and achievement. This chapter is your compass and roadmap, guiding you from the genesis of a goal to the gratifying pinnacle of its realization.

Establish the Goal:

You must first anchor your objective to set sail in the right direction. What is it that you yearn to accomplish? Picture it: a sales target that challenges yet inspires, a quota that stretches your capabilities without straining your resources. This goal is the lighthouse guiding your efforts through the tempestuous sales waters.

Necessary Materials and Prerequisites:

Before diving into the depths, ensure that your vessel is equipped. You'll need a clear understanding of your market, a comprehensive grasp of your product or service, and an unwavering commitment to the pursuit of excellence. Equip yourself with tools for tracking progress, such as CRM software, and resources for personal development, including books, courses, and mentors.

Begin with a Broad Overview:

Envision a tapestry where each thread is a step towards your ultimate goal. The broad overview is your sketch of this masterpiece. It comprises market analysis, client segmentation, and strategic planning—each pivotal in charting a course toward success.

Dive Into the Detailed Steps:

Now, let us unravel each thread, examining its texture and hue. Start by analyzing the market to understand where your opportunities lie. Segment your clients to tailor your approach to their unique needs. Devise a strategy that employs the strengths of your product or service to meet these needs. Break down your sales target into monthly, weekly, and daily objectives, making the insurmountable mountain a series of manageable hills. Some Tips and Warnings

Here's a nugget of wisdom: persistence is the twin of excellence. Do not waver when setbacks beckon; use them as stepping stones. Yet, tread carefully, for overzealous ambition can lead to burnout. Balance is key—harmonize your professional pursuits with personal well-being.

Validation:

How do you know when the sweet fruit of your labor is ripe for the picking? Measure, measure, measure. Keep a keen eye on your targets versus achievements. If your trajectory aligns with your plan, you're navigating true north. If not, adjust your sails.

Troubleshooting:

Encountered a squall? Perhaps clients are slipping through the net, or deals are stalling. Fear not. Revisit your approach, seek feedback, and refine your tactics. Remember, every problem is a disguised question begging for a solution.

As you stand at the precipice of action, let these words not simply wash over you but seep into the sinews of your ambition.

Are you prepared to elevate your purpose and turn goals into milestones? Will you allow the vigor of your vision to propel you forward?

The tapestry of achievement is vast, and the threads you weave today become the fabric of your tomorrow. Your goals are not just numbers on a spreadsheet; they are the milestones of your journey, the beacons of your growth. Each sale is not merely a transaction but a testament to your tenacity. So, ask yourself, what greatness are you willing to summon from within?

The path is laid out before you, a mosaic of opportunity and challenge. With every step, you'll craft a legacy in the annals of business and the essence of your life. For in the mastery of goal setting and achievement lies the secret to the next level!

Time Management for Sales Professionals

In the relentless pursuit of success, the scythe of time cuts through every intention, leaving behind either the blooms of achievement or the withered remnants of what could have been. The truth is stark yet simple: time, once gone, is beyond reclaim. For sales professionals, mastering time is not merely a skill but a formidable weapon in the arsenal of success. This chapter is dedicated to sculpting your minutes and hours into a masterpiece of efficiency, ensuring that every tick of the clock propels you closer to the zenith of your sales potential.

The objective here is unequivocal: to transform your relationship with time from constant chase to harmonious control. You will learn to navigate through the ticking tempest with the grace of a seasoned captain, turning the tides in your favor as you uncover hidden pockets of opportunity and elevate your productivity to unprecedented heights.

Before you embark on this transformative journey, gather your tools—digital or analog planners, a reliable time-tracking app, and a mindset poised for disciplined change. As you navigate the sea of time management, these are your compass and map, your sextant and stars.

Imagine the horizon, painted with the broad strokes of effective time management: prioritization, delegation, and strategic planning. This panoramic view is the prelude to the intricate dance of managing time—a dance where the steps are as necessary as the rhythm.

As we go deeper into the details, visualize your day as a series of blocks allocated to a specific purpose. Begin by categorizing tasks using the time-honored Eisenhower Matrix, sorting them into quadrants of urgency and importance. Next, embrace the potent practice of time-blocking, carving out segments of your day dedicated to proactive sales activities, client meetings, and administrative tasks.

But what of the unexpected, the tasks that ambush your agenda with the stealth of a shadow? Herein lies the art of flexibility within structure. Allocate buffer times—small oases of unscheduled moments—to absorb the shock of sudden demands.

Heed these tips as though the sages of sales whispered them:

Tackle the most daunting tasks when your energy crests like a wave in the morning. Guard your prime time zealously, for it is the crucible within which the gold of productivity is smelted. And remember the sharpening of the axe—continuous learning and skill enhancement—should never be forsaken for the sake of chopping more wood.

How will you know if your newfound mastery of time yields the harvest you seek? The proof is in the pulse of your productivity and the rhythm of your results. Track your activities, measure the outcomes against your goals, and watch your efficiency blossom.

Yet, even the most seasoned time-travelers may stumble upon temporal rifts. When distractions threaten to derail your day, or procrastination casts its paralyzing spell, confront these adversaries with the tenacity of a warrior. Reassess your methods, recalibrate your focus, and remember why you embarked on this journey— every moment is a step towards your Next Level Life.

Pause here and let the gravity of your quest sink in. Are you ready to wield time as your ally to carve out a legacy with each measured step? Do you feel the pulse of each second, each minute, urging you towards a life of designed purpose?

Time is the canvas, and your actions are the brushstrokes. With every disciplined decision, you paint the portrait of your professional prowess. Remember, the chronicles of history are not written in the ink of intention but in the bold, indelible lines of action. Will you harness the fleeting moments to etch your mark upon the tapestry of time?

The journey before you is one of discipline and determination, but the rewards are as boundless as time itself. Every tick is a drumbeat of progress, every tock a chime of opportunity. When measured not in hours but in accomplishments, your life becomes a symphony of purposeful existence. Take this step, and step into a realm where time is not an adversary but the most faithful of companions on your journey.

The Power of Habit in Sales

The sales profession is a testament to the power of influence and persuasion. Yet, beyond the surface of strategies and pitches lies an often-overlooked cornerstone of success: the power of habit. Top performers' consistent, daily practices are not born of happenstance but are the products of meticulously cultivated habits. As we unravel the tapestry of sales excellence, we find that at its very finest are the habits that shape and define the careers and lives of the most successful salespeople.

Habits, in their essence, are the routines we follow without conscious thought—the automatic actions and behaviors we perform daily. They are the invisible architecture of our lives, subtly sculpting our days and, consequently, our sales results. Understanding how to harness the power of habit can be the key to unlocking new levels of success in sales and beyond.

Consider the story of Jonathan, a sales professional whose career was transformed by the simple habit of daily planning. Each morning, without fail, he would spend thirty minutes outlining his goals, tasks, and the most strategic approach to his day's work. This habit kept him focused on his objectives and allowed him to anticipate challenges and opportunities. Over time, his consistent planning led to a remarkable improvement in his sales performance.

However, habits are not monolithic; they come in various shapes and serve different purposes. From the foundational habits that set the stage for productivity, such as sleep and exercise, to the specific sales-related habits, like following up with leads or personalizing customer interactions, each habit contributes to a repertoire of success.

Let us consider the insights of Charles Duhigg, who, in his seminal work "The Power of Habit," introduces the concept of the habit loop, comprising a cue, a routine, and a reward. Sales professionals can leverage this loop by identifying the cues that trigger productive behaviors, establishing routines that lead to successful outcomes, and ensuring that each routine is followed by a reward that reinforces the habit.

For instance, a salesperson might notice that they are most effective at making cold calls after their morning coffee—a cue that signals it's time to start their calling routine. The reward might be the satisfaction of checking off a significant number of calls from their to-do list or the thrill of securing a promising lead. Over time, this loop becomes second nature, and the habit of making calls becomes ingrained.

Diverse perspectives shed light on the power of habit in sales. Some experts emphasize the importance of "keystone habits," which are habits that have the power to start a chain reaction, changing other habits as they move through the loop. For a salesperson, a keystone habit might be the disciplined use of a CRM system, which can lead to better lead tracking, more efficient follow-ups, and, ultimately, more sales.

Data and facts support the transformative potential of good habits in sales. Research suggests that it takes, on average, 66 days for a new behavior to become automatic. Sales teams incorporating habit formation into their training programs often see a notable uptick in performance metrics, such as an increase in the number of calls made or deals closed.

When discussing complex concepts like habit formation and its psychological underpinnings, it's critical to clarify terms such as "habit loop" and "keystone habits." A habit loop is the cycle through which a habit becomes cemented in our behavior, and keystone habits are those that cause a domino effect, influencing several aspects of our behavior and leading to multiple positive outcomes.

In conclusion, cultivating positive sales habits is not a mere accessory to a sales professional's skill set; it is the engine that drives sustained performance and success. As we've explored, the power of habit in sales is multifaceted, touching on psychological patterns, the influence of keystone habits, and the impact of consistent daily routines. By intentionally fostering beneficial habits, sales professionals can elevate their craft to new heights, resulting in better sales outcomes and a more fulfilling professional journey.

As you close this chapter, reflect on the habits that underpin your sales activities. What routines can you establish or refine to enhance your sales performance? How can you create a habit loop that works to your advantage. Remember, the journey to harnessing the power of habit is one of persistence and patience.

But the rewards—a next-level selling experience and a next-level life—are well within your grasp. Embrace the challenge and let the transformative power of habit lead you to your pinnacle of sales excellence.

Avoiding Burnout: Balance and Recovery

In our relentless pursuit of professional excellence and the dizzying heights of sales success, we often overlook a perilous cliff that looms dangerously close—the cliff of burnout. Picture yourself in a boat, rowing with indefatigable vigor towards the island of achievement. Each stroke represents your hard work, late nights, and sacrificed weekends. But as you draw nearer, you fail to notice the water seeping into your vessel, the fatigue in your muscles, and the storm clouds gathering overhead. This is the current issue—the silent encroachment of burnout.

Burnout, the primary challenge we face, is not a sudden collapse but a gradual erosion of our well-being. It's the mental and emotional exhaustion, the cynicism, and the feeling of reduced personal accomplishment that professionals often experience. It's the engine of our ambition running hot, too hot, until it seizes.

If left unaddressed, the consequences are dire. The once vibrant salesperson, brimming with enthusiasm, may find themselves staring blankly at their screen, the numbers and names blurring into irrelevance. Relationships suffer at work and home, and the health that fuels our ambitions can falter, leading to a cascade of negative outcomes, personal and professional.

The solution? Balance and recovery. We must learn to set sails of self-care that catch the winds of our efforts, allowing us to glide forward rather than row in desperation. Balance is not about working less; it's about working smart and replenishing our reserves.

How do we implement this? First, we must establish boundaries. Determine when work begins and ends. Let technology be a tool, not a tether. Designate times to check emails and messages and stick to them. When your workday ends, step away physically and mentally. This might mean turning off notifications after a certain hour or having a ritual that signifies the end of professional time, like a walk or a specific playlist.

Next, integrate restorative practices into your routine. It could be as simple as taking short breaks throughout the day to stretch, breathe, or shift your focus. Incorporate activities that recharge you, be they physical exercise, meditation, or hobbies that have nothing to do with work.

But what evidence do we have that these strategies work?

Studies have shown that employees who maintain a clear separation between work and personal time report higher levels of job satisfaction and reduced burnout. Furthermore, companies that encourage a culture of balance often see lower turnover rates and higher productivity.

While these solutions are effective, they are not the only ones. Alternative strategies include delegating tasks, using productivity techniques like the Pomodoro Technique, or even seeking a change in environment or job role if the source of burnout is deeply embedded in the current one.

Imagine a sales team where every member operates from a place of balance. They work with intensity but also with joy and clarity. They challenge each other but support each other's need for recovery. The result is a healthier team and a more effective and resilient one.

Balance and recovery are not just strategies; they are commitments to a Next Level Life, where success in sales is not achieved at the expense of our well-being but is enhanced by it. So ask yourself, what boundaries will you set today? What practices will you integrate into your life to ensure your next level is not just a peak but a sustainable plateau?

In the words of the renowned author and my all-time favorite speaker, Jim Rohn, "Take care of your body. It's the only place you have to live." Let this be your mantra as you navigate the waters of your career. Balance your vessel, recover your strength, and let the island of achievement come to you, not as a conqueror to a prize but as a traveler to a home that promises success and serenity.

Discipline Vs. Disappointment: A Comparative Analysis

Much like a master-crafted mosaic, the art of sales is composed of countless pieces, each with its unique hue and shape. When assembled with meticulous care and deliberate intent, the image that arises is one of success—grand and undeniable. This brings us to examine two contrasting methodologies within the sales world: the disciplined approach and its unruly counterpart, the undisciplined method.

Within the sales world, discipline emerges as the bedrock upon which towering careers are built. The invisible yet palpable force propels the salesperson from the depths of potential to the zenith of achievement. Conversely, the lack of discipline is akin to setting sail without a compass, a journey fraught with uncertainty and ripe for disappointment. Our aim here is to dissect these methodologies, to understand the fibers that compose their being, and to glean insights that might illuminate the path forward for those who seek to excel not only in sales but in life itself.

What criteria, then, shall we use to judge these two approaches? We must consider their impact on productivity, customer relationships, goal attainment, and personal well-being. This framework will serve as our analytical compass, guiding us through the intricate webs of habit and consequence that define disciplined and undisciplined strategies in sales.

When observing the disciplined salesperson, one notes a striking consistency. Like a seasoned gardener who attends to their crops with unwavering regularity, the disciplined seller also cultivates their leads, nurtures client relationships, and prunes their pipeline with care. In this garden, there is no weed of procrastination, no drought of neglect. The disciplined approach, therefore, shares the similarity of order and predictability across the spectrum of successful sales professionals.

In stark contrast, the undisciplined approach lacks this structure. Here, the sales landscape is overgrown with the vines of missed opportunities and the brambles of last-minute rushes. The undisciplined seller may, at times, stumble upon a bloom of success, but these are fleeting and often the result of serendipity rather than strategy.

Visual aids, while not present in this textual format, could easily depict the disciplined approach with a steady, ascending line, while the undisciplined approach might resemble a volatile stock chart— peaks and valleys in unpredictable succession.

The analysis of these two methodologies reveals that discipline is not merely a set of actions but a mindset. It is the quiet resolve that filters distractions and sharpens focus. It is the unwavering commitment to a process that has proven effective, even when the allure of shortcuts and procrastination beckons. Discipline, in essence, is the architect of a salesperson's success and the guardian of their well-being.

In the contemporary sales world, this conversation is more than theoretical; it is urgently relevant. We live in an era of unparalleled distractions, where technology offers both the gift of connectivity and the curse of constant interruption. The disciplined salesperson utilizes technology as a lever for efficiency, while the undisciplined individual becomes ensnared in a web of unproductive activity.

So, where do you see yourself in this analysis? Have you cultivated the garden of your career with the steady hand of discipline, or have you left your potential to the whims of an undisciplined approach? Reflect upon this, for the answer holds the key to your success in sales and the quality of your life beyond the office walls.

Consider this poignant question: Are your daily habits propelling you towards a vision of excellence, or are they ensnaring you in the undergrowth of mediocrity? The power of discipline lies in its ability to transform the latter into the former, turning what was once a tangled mess into a pathway of clarity.

In conclusion, let us remember that discipline is not the adversary of freedom but its greatest ally. Through discipline, we gain the freedom to achieve, the freedom to excel, and ultimately, the freedom to live a Next Level Life. As the ancient philosopher Aristotle once said, "We are what we repeatedly do. Excellence, then, is not an act but a habit." Let us choose to make excellence our habit, discipline our method, and succeed in our inevitable destination.

CHAPTER 3

CREATING IRRESISTIBLE CONNECTIONS

The Art of Persuasion

I n the world of sales and beyond, the power to persuade is akin to holding the keys to a kingdom. It is not about deceit or manipulation; instead, it's an art form that, when mastered, can unlock doors to new opportunities and foster connections that enrich both your professional and personal life.

The concept of persuasion is ancient, yet it remains as relevant today as it was in the times of Aristotle, who outlined the modes of persuasion: ethos, pathos, and logos. Ethos appeals to ethics, pathos to emotions, and logos to logic. Mastering these three pillars can transform how you communicate, but it requires a nuanced approach that avoids confrontation and invites collaboration.

To truly understand the art of persuasion, consider the case of a seasoned salesperson who never seems to be selling at all. Clients flock to them, not because they feel pressured but because they feel understood. This salesperson knows that persuasion is not about pushing a product but about presenting a solution to a need, a key to a problem. They use examples and stories that resonate with their clients, illustrating the value of what they offer in a way that is both tangible and relatable.

Imagine a young couple looking to buy their first home. They are unsure and hesitant amid a sea of options and financial considerations. A real estate agent, skilled in the art of persuasion, doesn't just list the features of a house. Instead, they paint a picture of life in that home: the smell of coffee in the morning sundrenched kitchen, the laughter of friends gathered around the backyard fire pit, and the security of a neighborhood where children ride bikes until dusk. The agent isn't selling a house; they're selling a dream, a lifestyle, a future.

From another perspective, consider the non-profit organizer rallying support for a cause. They weave statistics into compelling narratives, making each number a testament to the urgency and impact of their mission. They know that facts alone can be cold, but facts told through stories ignite action. They don't just ask for donations; they offer a chance to be part of a movement, make a difference, and change lives.

At times, the art of persuasion involves clarifying complex terms, making them accessible to all. Take the financial advisor who demystifies investment terms, breaking them down into simple analogies. They don't discuss "diversification" in abstract terms; they compare it to planting a varied garden, where different crops thrive in different seasons, ensuring a bountiful harvest year-round.

As we dig deeper into this subject, let's not forget the importance of key takeaways. Remember that persuasion is more about connection than coercion. It's about finding common ground and speaking to shared values. It's about listening actively and responding with solutions that resonate personally.

Moreover, it's about trust, built on a foundation of authenticity and reinforced with every interaction.

By now, perhaps you're envisioning yourself weaving the subtle threads of persuasion into your interactions. Have you considered what opportunities might unfold if you approached your next negotiation not as a battle to be won but as a puzzle to be solved together? Can you see the difference it would make if you shifted your focus from selling a product to providing a service, from highlighting features to offering benefits?

In conclusion, the art of persuasion is not about winning arguments or forcing agreements; it is about guiding others to see your perspective's value, feel understood, and join you on a journey to mutual satisfaction willingly. Whether in sales, leadership, or everyday life, mastering this art can indeed elevate you to the next level—professionally and personally.

So, as you turn the page, ask yourself: How will I apply the subtle art of persuasion to my next interaction? How will it transform my approach to selling, leading, and living a next-level life? Applying the art of persuasion has undoubtedly changed my life!

Building Rapport With Prospects

Connecting with potential customers is an intricate dance—a blend of art and science, empathy and strategy. As you turn the page from understanding the subtle art of persuasion, the next step in your journey toward next-level selling and a next-level life is mastering the skill of building rapport with prospects. This isn't just about making an excellent first impression; it's about forging a genuine connection that paves the way for trust, communication, and, ultimately, a successful sale.

Your goal here is clear: establishing a relationship with your prospects built on understanding and mutual respect. This connection will serve as the foundation for all future interactions, making it easier for you to address their needs and for them to see the value in what you offer.

Before you dive into the nuances of rapport-building, ensure you're equipped with the necessary materials: an open mind, active listening skills, empathy, and patience. These are the prerequisites for creating a genuine connection with anyone, and they are particularly crucial when your objective is to foster a business relationship.

Take a moment to envision the roadmap we're about to navigate together. It begins with research and preparation, moves through the initial contact, and progresses into maintaining the relationship long-term. This overview might seem deceptively simple, but each part of the process is layered with complexities and subtleties that you'll learn to navigate with finesse.

Let's get into the detailed steps of building rapport with your prospects:

1. Before meeting with a prospect, do your homework. Gather information about their business, industry, and interests, if possible. This knowledge will inform your conversation and demonstrate your genuine interest in their world.

2. First impressions are powerful. Start by offering a warm greeting, a smile, and a firm handshake. Pay attention to the nonverbal cues you're both sending and receiving. Mirroring their body language can subtly create a sense of alignment and comfort.

3. Discover shared interests or experiences. This could be as simple as discussing a mutual love for a sport or as complex as finding commonality in business challenges. Whatever the shared interest, it serves as a bridge between you and the prospect.

4. Listen more than you speak. Show that you are interested in what they have to say by maintaining eye contact, nodding, and asking follow-up questions. This

demonstrates respect and a willingness to understand their perspective.

5. Let them know you appreciate their challenges and triumphs. Empathy builds trust, and trust is the currency of rapport.

6. Provide insights, advice, or even a helpful contact. Offering value without an immediate expectation of return positions you as a resource, not just a salesperson.

7. Send a personalized message referencing something specific from your conversation after your initial meeting. This reinforces the connection and keeps the lines of communication open.

Offering tips and warnings along this journey is crucial. Remember to be genuine; people can sense insincerity from a mile away. Avoid dominating the conversation or steering it back to your product too quickly. The rapport-building stage is about them, not you or your offering.

Testing or validation comes in the form of reciprocal communication. You'll know you've successfully built rapport when your prospect is open and responsive, seeks your opinion, and shares information with you that goes beyond surface-level pleasantries.

If you encounter troubleshooting scenarios, such as a prospect who remains distant despite your efforts, don't force it. Instead, give them space and try a different approach later. Sometimes, rapport takes time to develop, and patience can be your greatest ally.

As you refine your ability to build rapport, consider this vivid imagery: Imagine each prospect as a book with a unique story. Your job is not to write their story for them but to read it, understand it, and perhaps add a chapter that enriches it. Can you see yourself sitting across from a prospect, not as a salesperson, but as a curious reader eager to learn and contribute to their narrative?

Incorporating these techniques into your sales strategy isn't just about improving your numbers—it's about enhancing your life. When you connect with people, you open doors to new opportunities, friendships, and experiences. You transform not just your sales approach but your worldview.

So, as you reflect on the steps outlined here, ask yourself: How can I apply these principles to my next prospect meeting? How will building rapport advance my career and enrich my life experiences? Remember, when you elevate your connections, you elevate your life. Welcome to the next level!

Understanding the Customer Journey

Understanding the customer journey is akin to navigating a labyrinth's intricate twists and turns. Each step the customer takes is part of a larger story, a narrative that, when fully grasped, offers invaluable insights into tailoring your approach to their unique needs and desires. This understanding serves as the compass that guides your sales strategy, leading to a more profound connection with your clients and, consequently, a more fulfilling life.

Imagine embarking on a voyage across the vast ocean. Just as a seasoned sailor reads the stars to chart their course, a skilled salesperson must read their customer's signals to navigate the purchasing process effectively. The customer journey is the constellation of touchpoints, from the initial awareness of a need to the post-purchase reflections.

Consider the tale of a young couple searching for their first home. They begin with a dream, an image of a cozy hearth, and a backyard for future children to play. This dream sparks their journey, leading them to research neighborhoods, visit open houses, and consult real estate agents. Each interaction, each piece of information, builds upon their vision and shapes their decision- making process.

Now, translate this to your sales approach. By mapping out the customer's journey, you become the trusted guide, the real estate agent who understands their dream and the pitfalls and peaks of the journey itself. You are not just selling a product or service; you are facilitating a quest, helping the customer to reach their ultimate destination—a solution that resonates with their innermost aspirations.

But why does this matter? Data shows that customers who enjoy positive experiences are likelier to become repeat buyers, recommend your services to others, and form a lasting bond with your brand. According to a study by the Temkin Group, companies that earn $1 billion annually can expect to earn, on average, an additional $700 million within three years of investing in customer experience.

To clarify any complex terms, consider "customer experience" as the total of all customer interactions with your brand, from the first advertisement they see to the support they receive after making a purchase. It encompasses every touchpoint, every moment of engagement, and every opportunity you have to make an impression.

As we draw this chapter close, let us crystallize the key takeaways. Understanding the customer's journey allows you to anticipate needs, personalize interactions, and build a lasting connection that goes beyond the transactional. It's about recognizing that each customer is the hero of their own story, and you have the honor of being part of that narrative.

So, as you turn the page on this chapter, ask yourself: How well do I understand the journey my customers are on? How can I illuminate the path ahead, not just for their sake, but to elevate my own life to the next level? Embrace the journey, for in doing so, you unlock the door to Next Level Selling—and your Next Level Life.

The Role of Empathy in Sales

In the intricate dance of sales, there is one partner whose steps are often misunderstood yet crucial to the performance—the concept of empathy. Picture yourself in a bustling marketplace, the commotion of voices vying for attention, each stallholder convinced of the superiority of their wares. Imagine a vendor who leans in to listen and truly understand each passerby's needs and desires instead of shouting louder. This vendor is practicing the art of empathy, a subtle yet powerful tool in the salesperson's arsenal.

What exactly is empathy? Simply put, it is the ability to understand and share the feelings of another. It's a step beyond sympathy, which is feeling compassion for someone; empathy is placing yourself in someone else's shoes, seeing through their eyes, and feeling with their heart. It's a quality that enables us to connect with others more deeply.

Diving deeper, empathy in sales involves key elements such as active listening, emotional intelligence, and genuine curiosity. Active listening requires giving full attention to the prospective buyer, acknowledging their concerns, and responding thoughtfully. Emotional intelligence is the ability to perceive and manage your emotions and those of your customers. Genuine curiosity is the desire to know more about the person you are engaging with beyond the immediate transaction.

The roots of empathy can be traced back to the Greek word "empathia," meaning 'in emotion,' and has evolved through various philosophical and psychological interpretations to the nuanced understanding we have today. It's not merely a feeling; it's a cognitive function that has been studied and revered as a bridge between individuals, fostering understanding and trust.

Placing empathy within the broader framework of sales, we see it as a cornerstone of customer-centric selling. This approach prioritizes the customer's needs and experiences and hinges on the ability to truly understand what drives their decisions, concerns, and preferences.

How does this manifest in real-world scenarios? Consider a financial advisor who, rather than immediately selling the most profitable investment package, first seeks to understand the client's long-term goals, fears about risk, and personal values. This advisor uses empathy to provide tailored advice that resonates personally, building a trusting relationship that will likely endure over time.

One common misconception is that empathy is an inherent trait that cannot be developed. On the contrary, it is a skill that can be honed with practice and intention. Sales professionals can cultivate empathy by engaging in role-playing exercises, seeking feedback, and reflecting on their interactions with clients.

Let us paint a vivid picture. Imagine the world through the eyes of a prospect. They navigate a labyrinth of choices, bombarded by features, benefits, and offers. Through the empathetic lens, you see a potential sale and a person seeking guidance, reassurance, and validation of their concerns. You perceive the subtle furrow of their brow, the hopeful glint in their eye, and the cautious optimism in their voice. Your response is not a pre-packaged pitch but a tailored conversation acknowledging their unique situation.

Have you ever considered how deeply empathy can impact your sales approach? By truly engaging with your prospects, you elevate the sales experience and pave the way for a more meaningful and fulfilling professional life. Your interactions become less about the transaction and more about the transformation—yours and your client's.

Incorporate this reflective question: When was the last time someone truly understood you? The warmth and connection from that experience is what you aim to recreate in every sales encounter.

Let us conclude with a potent, one-line truth: Empathy in sales is not about manipulation but connection. By mastering this art, you achieve better sales results and contribute to a culture of understanding and respect, reinforcing the very fabric of a Next Level Life.

As we turn the final page of this chapter, let us commit to empathy, a promise to see beyond the surface and engage with the hearts and minds of those we serve. In doing so, we unlock the potential for more tremendous sales success and richer, more authentic human connections—the true essence of Next Level Selling.

Non-Verbal Communication Cues

In the sales world, the power of words is widely acknowledged. Yet, an unspoken force is equally at play, shaping the contours of our interactions and often determining the success or failure of a deal. This force is non-verbal communication, a repertoire of gestures, expressions, and postures that speak volumes without uttering a single word. As we delve into the realm of body language and other non-verbal cues, we uncover the tools to build stronger, more intuitive connections with our clients and peers.

The potency of non-verbal communication lies in its subtlety and its universality. Across cultures and industries, our bodies are broadcasting messages, many of which we aren't consciously aware of. But by harnessing this knowledge, we step into a level of mastery that elevates our sales approach, transforming it into an art form that resonates on a deeper, more instinctual level.

Let's examine the critical components of non-verbal communication that can refine our interactions and forge indelible bonds:

1. Facial Expressions
2. Eye Contact
3. Posture and Stance
4. Gestures
5. Proximity and Personal Space
6. Touch
7. Tone of Voice

Facial Expressions

The human face is a canvas of complexity, capable of conveying many emotions without a single spoken word. Our expressions can mirror our innermost feelings, betray our doubts, or amplify our confidence. When engaging with clients, the subtle play of our facial muscles can lay the groundwork for trust and rapport.

Consider the warmth conveyed by a genuine smile that crinkles the eyes and lights up the face. This simple gesture can act as a bridge, connecting us to others. Conversely, a furrowed brow or a fleeting frown might signal concern or disagreement, allowing us to adjust our approach further or delve into a topic.

Evidence from psychological studies suggests that people are more likely to do business with individuals whom they perceive as friendly and approachable, qualities often judged by their facial expressions. Sales professionals can leverage this by being mindful of their expressions and practicing in front of a mirror or recording themselves during mock sales pitches.

Practical applications of this knowledge are abundant. Imagine adjusting your facial expressions to mirror those of your client subtly. This technique, known as mirroring, has increased empathy and understanding, paving the way for a more connected conversation.

Eye Contact

The eyes are not only windows to the soul but also conduits of credibility and confidence. Maintaining appropriate eye contact signifies that you are fully present and engaged, conveying respect for the person you are communicating with.

However, the key lies in balance. Unwavering, intense eye contact can be perceived as aggressive, while too little can be read as disinterest or lack of confidence. The art of eye contact is mastering the ebb and flow of your gaze, knowing when to hold it and when to look away gently.

Research in the field reveals that maintaining eye contact between 60% and 70% of the time during a conversation strikes the right chord, fostering a sense of connection and attentiveness.

In practice, when you lock eyes as a client articulates their needs, you're not just hearing them but showing them they have your undivided attention. It's a non-verbal nod of understanding that can make all the difference in a negotiation.

Posture and Stance

The way we carry ourselves sends signals about our mindset and intent. Standing tall with an open stance suggests confidence and openness, inviting others into our space. Conversely, crossed arms or a slumped posture can be interpreted as defensive or uninterested.

Sales professionals can capitalize on this by consciously adopting a posture that exudes confidence and receptivity. Aligning your posture with your message strengthens the impact of your words, creating a harmonious impression that can help seal the deal.

Gestures

Gestures can emphasize a point, signal enthusiasm, or convey sincerity. The key is to ensure that your gestures complement your verbal message rather than distract from it. Controlled, purposeful movements can underscore your points and add dynamism to your interactions.

Proximity and Personal Space

The physical distance we keep varies based on cultural norms and individual preferences. Respecting personal space is paramount, but leaning in slightly can express interest and engagement. Observing and mirroring your client's comfort with proximity can enhance the sense of connection.

Touch

When appropriate, a handshake, a pat on the back, or a light touch on the arm can humanize a business interaction. These small contacts can reinforce a point or signal agreement, fostering a sense of camaraderie and cooperation.

Tone of Voice

The inflections, pitch, and volume of our voice carry emotional weight. A warm, steady tone can soothe anxieties, while a passionate pitch can inspire and motivate. Attuning your vocal delivery to the context and content of your conversation can make your message resonate more deeply.

As we weave through this intricate tapestry of non-verbal communication, we see a common thread: the importance of congruence. Our non-verbal signals must align with our words to build trust and credibility. It's a dance of subtlety and strategy that requires practice, awareness, and a keen eye for the unspoken.

So, as you navigate the nuanced world of sales, remember the silent power of your presence. Embrace the unspoken cues that can elevate your interactions from mere transactions to transformative experiences. Master the art of non-verbal communication, and you will enhance your sales effectiveness and enrich the fabric of your connections, both professionally and personally.

In closing, ponder this: Are your non-verbal cues in harmony with the message you wish to convey? The answer to this question could very well be the key to unlocking the next level of your selling—and living—potential.

Storytelling as a Sales Tool

Imagine entering a room, the air buzzing with anticipation, as you prepare to deliver a pitch that could change the course of your career. You've got the facts, the figures, the features, and the benefits down pat. But there's an ace up your sleeve, a timehonored technique that has swayed hearts and minds since the dawn of humanity: storytelling. You're not just here to sell a product or service; you're here to weave a narrative that will captivate, resonate, and, ultimately, persuade.

Establish the Goal:

Your objective is clear. You aim to master the art of storytelling in sales, transforming your pitches into compelling narratives that inform and inspire your audience to act.

Necessary Materials and Prerequisites:

Before embarking on this journey, you'll need a few essentials. Gather knowledge of your product or service, insights into your target audience, a grasp of the essential elements of a story (character, setting, conflict, and resolution), and a willingness to practice and refine your technique.

Begin with a Broad Overview:

The roadmap to harnessing storytelling in sales involves understanding your audience, crafting a relatable protagonist, structuring your story, employing emotion, and confidently delivering your narrative.

The Detailed Steps:

First, know your audience. Demographics, pain points, and desires are the colors with which you'll paint your story. Next, create a protagonist who mirrors your audience's challenges, someone they can root for. Then, structure your story: set the stage, introduce the conflict, build tension, and arrive at a satisfying resolution where your product or service plays the hero. Weave in emotional threads that tug at the heartstrings; these hooks will keep your audience engaged. Finally, deliver your story with the conviction of a believer, for a tale told half-heartedly is a tale half- heard.

Some Tips and Warnings:

Remember, authenticity reigns supreme. Avoid fabricating stories or over-dramatizing. Also, be mindful of cultural sensitivities and steer clear of stereotypes. And don't let your story overshadow the core message; it should enhance, not eclipse.

Testing or Validation:

You'll know your storytelling has hit the mark when your audience is nodding along, when you see the spark of connection in their eyes, and when they come to you, eager to be part of the story you've told.

Troubleshooting:

If your story fails to resonate, revisit the elements. Maybe the conflict wasn't compelling, or the resolution was too vague. Adjust, refine, and try again.

The air of anticipation transforms into rapt attention as you begin. "Imagine," you say, and the room leans in. You're not listing features but embarking on a journey with them. The protagonist, like them, faces a familiar struggle. The tension rises; they feel it; they've been there. And just when all seems lost, a revelation: your product, the hero's blade, the key to unlocking their potential.

You weave the tale with a flourish, but your words are measured and carefully chosen. A vivid imagery here, a one-liner there, striking the balance between simplicity and depth. Your sentences ebb and flow an almost musical cadence punctuated by the occasional question that invites them to imagine themselves in the story.

As you conclude, a hush falls. You've taken them on an emotional rollercoaster, and now they stand as potential customers and characters who've lived the story. They see themselves in the narrative, and the product you sell is no longer just an item or a service; it's the key to their happily ever after.

You've done more than sell; you've told a story that entwines with their own. In doing so, you've reached the next level in selling and invited your clients to live their next-level lives, with your offering as a pivotal chapter in their ongoing stories.

From Prospect to Partner: The Evolution of a Sale

The journey from prospect to partner is an evolution as intricate as any tale of transformation. This is a story not of transactions but of relations, not of sales but of bonds. As we peel back the layers of time, we witness the metamorphosis of a singular event— a sale—into a saga of enduring partnership.

Our tale begins in the annals of trade history, where barter systems ruled, and trust was the currency of survival. Here, the earliest origins of selling were nurtured, sprouting from the necessity to exchange goods for mutual benefit. But this was merely the overture of a much grander symphony that would unfold over centuries.

Moving forward chronologically, we trace the milestones that have shaped the face of selling. The invention of currency gave rise to the concept of value, offering a more standardized method of exchange. Markets and fairs in medieval times turned selling into a social endeavor, where relationships began to influence trade. Fast forward to the Industrial Revolution, the advent of mass production transformed selling into a volume-driven practice, where the personal touch began to wane.

Yet, amidst these changes, a divergence appeared. Some astute sellers recognized that beyond the one-time deal lay a field ripe with opportunity—the potential for partnership. They understood that every handshake could sow the seeds for a lasting alliance, every exchange could be watered with trust, and every satisfied client could grow into a steadfast partner.

In this evolution, cultural and regional variations have played their parts. In the East, for instance, the concept of 'Guanxi'—a system of social networks and influential relationships—highlights the importance of personal connections in business dealings. Meanwhile, Western cultures often emphasize contractual agreements, underscoring the legalities that bind partnerships.

The modern interpretation of this evolutionary journey is both complex and fascinating. Today, we observe a renaissance of relationship-based selling fueled by technological advancements that allow for more personalized interactions. Customer Relationship Management (CRM) systems and social media platforms enable sellers to maintain close contact with clients, turning what used to be a cold call into a warm conversation.

But this path has not been without its challenges and controversies. The digital age brought about concerns about data privacy and the depersonalization of customer interactions. The turning point, however, lies in the realization that technology is a tool, not a replacement for the human element at every partnership's heart.

As we dive deeper into the details, let's visualize this transformation through a hypothetical diagram. In this spectrum, the left end marks the 'Prospect' stage, and the right end is the 'Partner' phase. In between, numerous touchpoints represent the key moments of interaction that foster trust and loyalty.

Ask yourself, where does your current approach lie on this spectrum? Are your sales strategies nurturing prospects toward partnership, or are they stuck in the transitory realm of transactions?

In your quest to evolve your selling strategy, remember that the strongest partnerships are built on a foundation of shared values and mutual respect. They are not formed overnight but crafted through consistent, genuine engagement. In the words of a seasoned sales veteran, "The deal is just the beginning. The true art lies in what happens after the handshake."

As we conclude this chapter, let the narrative of your selling journey echo the wisdom of the past and the innovations of the present. Embrace the challenges as opportunities to strengthen your resolve and celebrate each milestone as a testament to your commitment to moving from prospect to partner.

In the end, the essence of a sale is not captured in the exchange of goods or services but in the enduring relationships that are forged in its wake. And it is in these relationships that you find not just the evolution of a sale but the elevation of life itself.

CHAPTER 4

HOPE IS NOT A STRATEGY: TACTICAL SALES PLANNING

Developing a Proactive Sales Plan

I n the dynamic sales arena, the art of proactive planning can be the dividing line between ongoing success and the static state of mediocrity. 'Next Level Selling - Next Level Life' pivots on this axis of preemptive strategy, guiding you not just to another plateau but to a summit of sales mastery and personal fulfillment. As we embark on the chapter "Developing a Proactive Sales Plan," your journey will take you through a tapestry of meticulous preparation, actionable strategies, and the crystallization of your sales objectives.

At the heart of your ascension lies the goal—your beacon in the competitive storm. This chapter's mission is to arm you with the knowledge to craft a sales plan that is not reactive but charged with intent and direction. A plan that, once implemented, will set a course so unwavering that your sales targets become not just attainable but inevitable.

Before we dive into the intricacies of your master plan, let's inventory what you'll need to begin. A clear understanding of your product or service is paramount, as is an intimate knowledge of your target market. You will require tools for tracking progress, such as a customer relationship management (CRM) system and metrics for measuring success. An open mind, resilience, and the willingness to adapt are less tangible yet equally essential prerequisites.

Imagine, if you will, a broad canvas upon which the stages of your sales plan are about to be painted. The initial sketch outlines the sales objectives and explores your target market. Then, a detailed strategy for engagement is etched, culminating in a robust mechanism for feedback and adaptation.

Let's take the plunge into these details, the sinews that will hold your plan together. First, setting sales objectives is not simply about numbers; it's about aligning your aspirations with the practicalities of the market. Define clear, measurable, and time-bound goals. Then, research your target market as if you were an archaeologist uncovering civilizations—know their needs, desires, and pain points. This knowledge is power; the precision guides your arrow to its target.

Once your objectives and market understanding are in place, strategize your approach. How will you engage with your prospects? What channels will you use? Consider the customer journey and plot every touchpoint with the meticulousness of a cartographer mapping uncharted territories.

Now, take heed of these pearls of wisdom. Relationships are the currency of sales; invest in them wisely. Your integrity is not a card to be played but the hand holding all cards. And remember, a 'no' today might be a 'yes' tomorrow—perseverance is your ally.

But how will you know you've hit the mark? The truth lies in the evidence of your sales figures and customer feedback. Regularly review your metrics. Are you on track to meet your goals? Listen to what the data tells you, and let it refine your approach.

On occasion, the path may deviate; obstacles will emerge. Should you find that despite your best efforts, the results are wanting, don't despair. Troubleshoot by revisiting each step of your plan. Is your target market responding as expected? Are your engagement strategies effective? Adjust, pivot, and press on.

In sales, as in life, the beauty of the landscape is revealed through the climb. With each step in your proactive sales plan, you are not just selling a product or a service; you are offering a piece of a dream—yours and your customers. The summit awaits, but remember, the ascent forges the view.

So, are you ready to take that first step? To commit to a plan that is as proactive as it reflects your ambition? Let's climb this mountain together, and with each chapter, you'll find your footing surer, your gaze steadier, and your resolve firmer. 'Next Level Selling - Next Level Life' is not just a book; it's a manifesto for the relentless pursuit of excellence. And it begins with a plan—a proactive sales plan.

Market Analysis and Segmentation

Understanding who you are selling to is as crucial as knowing how to sell. In the bustling marketplaces of today's world, a keen ability to dissect and comprehend your audience can make the difference between a message that resonates and one that falls on deaf ears. Thus, we focus on the science and art of market analysis and segmentation, the bedrock upon which targeted sales approaches are built.

Imagine entering a room filled with potential customers with unique preferences, needs, and desires. Your task is not to broadcast a single message in the hope it will stick but to tailor your approach to the individual whispers of each prospect. To do this effectively, we must first segment our market and categorize it into manageable slices that share common characteristics and are likely to respond similarly to our marketing efforts.

The cornerstone of market analysis is the collection and interpretation of data that illuminates who your customers are. Demographics, psychographics, behavioral patterns, and geographic locations are not mere data points; they are the compass that guides your sales strategy. To substantiate this claim, consider the success stories of companies that have mastered the art of segmentation. They demonstrate increased engagement rates, higher conversion, and a more robust bottom line.

However, to delve deeper, one must consider that market segmentation is not a one-size-fits-all solution. It requires a nuanced approach. A business-to-business (B2B) software provider, for example, may segment their market by industry, company size, or decision-maker seniority. In contrast, a fashion retailer might segment their market by age, lifestyle, or even fashion sensibilities.

The skeptics might argue that segmentation can lead to overspecialization in a hyper-connected world, potentially alienating customers who don't fit neatly into a predefined segment. They warn against the pitfalls of pigeonholing customers, suggesting that such tactics may ignore the fluidity of consumer identity.

However, the rebuttal to this counterargument lies in the dynamic nature of segmentation itself. Effective market analysis is not a static process but an ongoing conversation with your market. It demands continuous reevaluation and adaptation, ensuring that no customer need goes unmet.

In some cases, additional supporting evidence may come from emerging data analytics and artificial intelligence (AI) trends. These technologies allow for micro-segmentation, where prospects can be understood and targeted at an individual level, thus addressing over-generalization concerns.

As we draw toward a conclusion, it is essential to reinforce the assertion that market analysis and segmentation are indispensable tools in the arsenal of any sales strategy. They afford us the clarity to see our market as a mosaic of opportunities, each segment a piece of the larger picture.

With this foundation laid, the subsequent chapters will build upon these concepts, teaching you how to engage each segment in a personal and genuine manner. But always remember, the market is a living entity, ever-changing and evolving. Your segmentation must be equally fluid, responsive to shifts in trends, and adaptable to new information.

So, let this knowledge be the lens through which you view your prospects. Each chapter will deepen your understanding, making your sales strategies more nuanced. Next Level Selling is about recognizing the individual in the crowd and speaking directly to them. It's about understanding that Next Level Life is achieved not through broad strokes but through carefully crafting messages that touch each unique customer's heart.

Are you prepared to dive into the depths of your market, to segment with skill, and to approach each prospect as an individual world unto themselves? Let's embark on this journey together and watch as the tapestry of your market unfolds into a clear and navigable map, leading you to sales success and personal achievement.

The Importance of Sales Metrics

In the ever-evolving sales landscape, the astute use of metrics guides strategies toward success. It's not just about having data but knowing which data points are the signposts to your destination— growth, efficiency, and, ultimately, a thriving business.

Before we get to the heart of the matter, let's take a moment to reflect on the importance of sales metrics. These figures and percentages are not mere numbers; they are the pulse of your business, indicative of its health and potential. You gain insight into performance, customer behavior, and market trends by measuring and analyzing them. But why is this so crucial?

Metrics are the foundation for building a robust and adaptable strategy. They tell you where you've been and where you stand and help chart the course for where you're headed. They are as much about predicting the future as they are about understanding the past.

With this understanding in mind, let us unveil the pivotal points that will be expanded upon in the following pages.

- Sales Volume
- Conversion Rate
- Customer Acquisition Cost (CAC)
- Customer Lifetime Value (CLV)
- Sales Cycle Length
- Lead Response Time
- Win Rate

Sales Volume

The heartbeat of any sales department is its sales volume—the sheer number of products or services sold within a given timeframe.

This metric offers a raw measure of output and market demand, a straightforward look at the vigor of your business activities.

To truly grasp sales volume, consider it a measure of effort and effectiveness. A high volume might indicate a thriving demand, a highly effective sales team, or both. Conversely, a dip can signal a need for strategic realignment or an indication of changing market conditions.

Evidence of the importance of sales volume can be found in countless case studies. For instance, a shift in sales volume can precede market trends, providing a company with the foresight to pivot before a downturn hits. It also serves as a leading indicator for revenue forecasting, inventory management, and capacity planning.

The practical application of tracking sales volume is multifaceted. It allows for better allocation of resources, targeted sales training, and can even inform marketing campaigns. A nuanced understanding of this metric enables businesses to adjust their sails before the wind changes, ensuring they always ride the wave, not capsizing beneath it.

Conversion Rate

The conversion rate is a testament to your sales funnel's effectiveness. This metric tells you the percentage of prospects who have taken the desired action—be it making a purchase, signing up for a newsletter, or scheduling a demo.

Imagine your sales process as a sieve; the conversion rate helps you understand the fineness of its mesh. A high conversion rate indicates a fine mesh adept at turning prospects into customers. A low rate, however, suggests that there are holes to be patched.

Real-life evidence of the power of conversion rate optimization is abundant. Consider the online retailer who tweaks its checkout process and sees a surge in sales or the SaaS company that refines its demo and witnesses an uptick in subscription sign-ups.

In practice, improving your conversion rate can be transformative. It can mean the difference between a floundering business and a flourishing one. It's about ensuring every touchpoint with a prospect is an opportunity to guide them toward saying "yes."

Customer Acquisition Cost (CAC)

The quest for new customers is an expensive endeavor, and the Customer Acquisition Cost (CAC) metric is your ledger, tallying the investment required to secure a new customer. It encompasses the total sales and marketing costs over a specific period, divided by the number of customers acquired.

Think of CAC as the price tag of your growth ambitions. A high CAC can be sustainable if balanced by high customer value, but it can also be a harbinger of inefficiency or overspending. It's a balancing act, ensuring that the cost of growth doesn't outstrip the benefits.

Evidence of CAC's importance can be found in the startup that reduced its CAC through targeted social media campaigns, resulting in improved profitability. Or in the company that discovered its CAC was too low, suggesting underinvestment in market opportunities.

Practical applications of CAC are evident in budget allocation, strategy formulation, and performance benchmarking. By understanding CAC, companies can decide where and how much to invest in customer acquisition efforts.

Customer Lifetime Value (CLV)

Customer Lifetime Value (CLV) is a forward-looking metric that predicts the total value your business can expect from a single customer account. It's a measure of the long-term worth of a customer, encompassing their entire relationship with your company.

CLV is the compass that points toward profitability. It helps determine how much you should invest in customer retention and informs strategies for upselling or cross-selling. A low CLV can signal a need for better customer engagement or improved product offerings.

Evidence of CLV's significance comes from businesses that have shifted their focus from short-term gains to long-term relationships, resulting in increased customer loyalty and revenue.

In practical terms, CLV influences decisions on customer service investments, loyalty programs, and personalized marketing efforts. It encourages businesses to foster relationships that are not just profitable but enduring.

Sales Cycle Length

The sales cycle length measures the time from the initial contact with a prospect to the closing of a sale. It's a timeline that encapsulates the efficiency of your sales process.

A shortened sales cycle suggests a streamlined, effective process, while a prolonged one can indicate bottlenecks or missed opportunities. Businesses can identify stages that need optimization for quicker conversions by analyzing the sales cycle.

Evidence of the importance of sales cycle length is seen in companies that have honed their sales process to reduce wait times, resulting in quicker revenue generation and improved customer satisfaction.

Understanding the sales cycle length enables better forecasting, resource allocation, and sales staff performance evaluation. It's about ensuring that time—your most precious resource—is utilized to its fullest.

Lead Response Time

Lead response time is a critical metric in a world where timing can be everything. It measures the speed at which your sales team responds to inquiries or leads.

A swift response can differentiate between securing a sale and losing it to a competitor. Evidence suggests that the probability of converting a lead decreases exponentially with each passing minute.

Practically, a focus on reducing lead response time can lead to improved conversion rates and customer satisfaction. It's about demonstrating to your prospects that their business is valued and that your company is attentive and agile.

Win Rate

Finally, the win rate gives you a clear picture of your successes versus your attempts. It's the percentage of deals closed compared to the number of deals initiated.

A high win rate is a cause for celebration, a testament to the effectiveness of your sales team and strategy. A low win rate, however, is a call to action, a prompt to reevaluate your approach.

Evidence of the win rate's impact is visible in businesses that have refined their sales tactics, leading to more closed deals and higher revenue.

In practical terms, the win rate is a performance indicator for sales teams, a metric to aspire to, and a measure to surpass. It's about turning opportunities into victories, time and again.

As we transition from one metric to the next, let's keep our eyes on the prize: a sales strategy that is not just functional but formidable. A strategy that leverages the power of metrics to turn data into dollars and insights into action.

Are you ready to take your sales metrics to the next level and, with them, your business? Each metric is a steppingstone on the path to a Next Level Life—a life where success is not just hoped for but engineered.

Adapting to Market Changes

In an ever-shifting market, the winds of change are not just inevitable; they are a constant force, reshaping the commercial landscape with each gust. As sales professionals, our ability to harness these winds and adjust our sails accordingly can mean the difference between a thriving enterprise and one that is left floundering in the wake of progress.

The challenge we face is not trivial. We are tasked with navigating an environment where consumer behaviors, economic climates, and competitive tactics are in perpetual flux. Without a keen eye and a flexible strategy, we risk being blindsided by shifts that could have been anticipated and capitalized upon.

Should we fail to adapt, the consequences are manifold. Picture a once-booming business now struggling to stay afloat because it clung too tightly to outdated practices. Sales plummet, morale plummets and the once steady stream of satisfied customers reduces to a trickle. This is the bleak reality for those who ignore the telltale signs of market change.

But what if there were a way to survive these shifts and thrive because of them? What if we could pivot with precision and purpose, turning potential pitfalls into launching pads for success?

The solution lies in developing a dynamic sales plan that is as alive and responsive as the market itself. This plan must be rooted in a deep understanding of market indicators and customer feedback, allowing for swift and strategic adjustments.

Implementing such a solution begins with thoroughly analyzing current market trends and potential disruptors. Engage in regular dialogue with customers, conduct competitive analysis, and stay abreast of industry developments. Craft a sales plan that includes flexible pricing strategies, product or service adaptations, and contingency plans for various market scenarios from this foundation of knowledge.

Consider the story of a tech company that, noticing a shift towards mobile computing, pivoted from desktop software to mobile apps, thereby capturing a new and burgeoning market. Or the retailer who, observing the rise of e-commerce, embraced online sales and digital marketing, revitalizing its brand and expanding its reach.

Alternative solutions might include diversifying product lines, entering new markets, or even strategic partnerships to bolster resilience against market volatility. Each of these paths should be evaluated not just for their potential benefits but for their alignment with your business's core values and strengths.

Remember to keep your narrative engaging as you embark on this adaptation journey. Picture a ship's captain, eyes fixed on the horizon, adeptly steering through stormy seas, and ask yourself: Are you prepared to be that captain for your business? Can you spot the early signs of change and adjust your course accordingly?

Embrace a sales strategy that is as fluid as the market itself. Let each success story be a testament to your agility and each failure a lesson in the art of pivoting. By doing so, you're not just selling— you're ensuring the longevity and vitality of your business in a world where change is the only constant.

In the chapters ahead, we will delve deeper into the strategies that will empower you to meet the demands of an evolving marketplace and set the pace, becoming a beacon for others to follow. Prepare to embark on a journey towards a Next

Level Selling approach that will lead to a Next Level Life, where each market change is not a threat but an opportunity for growth and innovation.

Strategic Use of CRM Systems

A well-oiled machine is the dream of every visionary leader.

Imagine a robust system that keeps track of and nourishes your leads, a digital companion whispering the secrets of each client's desires into your ear. This is not the stuff of fantasy; this is the strategic use of CRM (Customer Relationship Management) systems, and it's your key to unlocking a streamlined sales process.

Establish the Goal

Your mission, should you choose to accept it, is to master the art of CRM to elevate your sales game. By the end of this chapter, you'll possess the knowledge to wield this powerful tool, turning potential chaos into a symphony of organized data and actionable insights.

Necessary Materials or Prerequisites:

Before you embark on this transformative journey, ensure you have:

1. A CRM system that aligns with your business size and complexity.

2. A clear understanding of your sales process and customer journey.

3. Buy-in from your team, who must utilize the system effectively.

4. Data from various sources can be centralized within your CRM.

Begin with a Broad Overview:

Imagine your sales process as a grand tapestry, each thread representing a client or lead. CRM is the loom that weaves these threads into a coherent picture. This tapestry begins with acquiring leads, followed by nurturing those relationships, forecasting sales, and analyzing data to refine your approach.

Dive into the Detailed Steps:

The first step is inputting your data, a meticulous yet critical phase. Populate your CRM with customer information, ensuring accuracy for a solid foundation. Next, segment your leads for targeted communication. Consider setting the stage for a play where each actor knows their role.

Now, engage with your leads. Schedule calls, send emails, and record every interaction. The CRM becomes your history repository, a chronicle of the budding relationship between you and your prospects.

As deals progress, use the CRM to forecast sales. This crystal ball of data lets you predict revenue and adjust your strategy accordingly.

Finally, analyze the results. Which tactics succeeded? Which faltered? Let the CRM guide you through these reflections.

Some Tips and Warnings:

Be wary of data entry errors; they can lead to misinformed decisions. Regularly clean your database to maintain its integrity. Engage your team through training and foster an environment where the CRM is seen as an ally, not a chore.

Testing or Validation:

You'll know you've succeeded when your sales process feels like a well-rehearsed ballet. Leads will flow smoothly through the pipeline, and your forecasting will become more accurate. Look for an uptick in customer satisfaction and retention as proof of the pudding.

Troubleshooting (optional)

If your team is resistant, demonstrate the CRM's value through small wins. When issues arise with the system, work closely with your provider—most complications are a stone's throw away from a solution.

The strategic use of CRM systems is not just about storing information; it's about transforming data into a competitive edge. It's about knowing your customers so intimately that each interaction is personalized and potent.

Does this sound like a system you have in place? If not, the time to act is now. Each day without a CRM is a day where opportunities might slip like sand through your fingers.

Picture this: a dashboard aglow with metrics, charts mapping your success, and the pulse of your business at your fingertips. This is what awaits you at the end of this CRM journey.

Simple language, direct questions, and vivid imagery aside, the message is clear. CRM is not just a tool; it's the lifeblood of modern selling. It's about nurturing relationships as if they were delicate blossoms in a garden of opportunity.

And so, as you turn the page, consider this not just another chapter in a book but a new chapter in your career. Embrace CRM with open arms and watch your sales process and life ascend to the next level.

Risk Management in Sales

Have you ever pondered the precipice of a deal where the potential for loss seems as vast as the opportunity for gain? It's the point where the art of selling teeters on the fine line of risk, where a misstep could mean a tumble into the abyss of missed targets and lost revenues. Welcome to the world of risk management in sales, where foresight meets strategy in a dance that could elevate your business to unforeseen heights or lead to an unceremonious fall.

In the bustling marketplace, risks lurk in the shadows of every transaction, every handshake. They are the silent deal-breakers that, if left unchecked, could unravel the tapestry of success you've so meticulously woven. In identifying and managing these risks, it is here that the future of your sales and, indeed, your life hangs in the balance.

Consider the multitude of uncertainties that a sales team might encounter: the sudden shift in consumer behavior, the emergence of a formidable competitor, or even the loss of a key account. Each of these situations can potentially disrupt the status quo, turning what was once a predictable outcome into a question mark.

But what if these risks go unmanaged? Picture a scenario where your sales forecast becomes as unreliable as a weather prediction in the tropics, where your team's morale plummets like a stone in water, and your market share shrinks as if washed away by an unforeseen storm. This is the grim portrait of a future without risk management.

Now, imagine a different scene, one where these risks are acknowledged and addressed with precision and confidence. Herein lies the solution: a proactive approach to risk management, one that involves identifying potential pitfalls, assessing their impact, and implementing strategies to mitigate or avoid them entirely.

The first step is creating a risk register, a living document that captures potential threats and their impacts. This becomes your map through the minefield of sales, guiding your decisions and strategies. Next, develop a set of contingency plans and realistic scenarios that prepare you for the worst while striving for the best. These lifeboats on your commerce ship are ready to be deployed when the waters get rough.

As you forge ahead, communication is the beacon that keeps your team aligned and informed. Regular updates on potential risks and the strategies in place to mitigate them will serve as the drumbeat to which your sales force marches. It's not just about being aware of the dangers; it's about being prepared to face them together.

But how do you know if these measures are working? Look to the past, to the lessons learned from deals that went south and from victories hard-won. And look to the future, to the trends and patterns that can inform your strategies. This is evidence of your solution's efficacy, proof that your ship can weather the storm and sail through it with unfurled sails.

Of course, there are alternative solutions and other routes one might take. Some prefer a more aggressive stance, pushing ahead with blind optimism, while others take a conservative approach, avoiding risk at the expense of opportunity. Each has its merits, but the balance lies in a calculated strategy that acknowledges the reality of risk without being paralyzed by its potential.

As you navigate through this chapter, let your mind's eye visualize the various scenarios presented. Let the questions posed resonate with your own experiences and aspirations. Are you prepared for the uncertainties that lie ahead? Is your team equipped to handle the inevitable challenges of the sales journey?

In crafting your risk management strategy, remember the power of simplicity. There is elegance in a plan that can be easily understood and executed and doesn't require a decoder to interpret. Let the rhythm and cadence of your actions reflect the fluidity and adaptability required in the face of adversity.

And so, as we close this section of our book, take a moment to reflect on the gravity of risk management in sales. It's not merely a chapter in a manual; it's a critical component of a next level selling strategy that could make the difference between a life of constant struggle and one of sustained success. Embrace the principles within these pages, and watch your sales and life reach new heights.

Case Studies: Strategic Sales Successes

In the competitive landscape of today's business world, strategic sales planning can often be the difference between barely surviving and thriving with momentum. It's a tale of precision, insight, and adaptability woven into the fabric of an organization's culture. Here, we will delve into a case study that encapsulates this ethos, offering a lens through which to view the intricate dance of sales strategy.

Our scene unfolds within the bustling tech industry, a realm where innovation is as constant as the northern star and competition as fierce as the midday sun. A mid-sized software company known for its cutting-edge solutions in cybersecurity had reached a precipice. Growth had plateaued, and the ever-increasing pressure from new market entrants was beginning to show cracks in their armor.

Enter the main players: the company's CEO, a visionary with an ironclad resolve, and the newly appointed Sales Director, a dynamo of strategic thinking with a track record of transforming underperforming sales teams. These figures stood at the helm, ready to steer the company through the storm.

The challenge was clear: rejuvenate the stagnating sales figures and reclaim market share from the encroaching competitors. The Sales Director quickly identified that the sales process was out of sync with the evolving needs of their clients. It was a puzzle that required a new piece and a whole new strategy to complete the picture.

The approach was multifaceted. First, they revamped the sales training program, incorporating methodologies that embraced consultative selling and value-based approaches. They equipped their sales force with data analytics tools to understand customer needs better and tailor their pitches accordingly. Next, they restructured the compensation plan to incentivize not just new client acquisition but also the nurturing of existing relationships.

As weeks turned into months, the results began to materialize. Sales figures rose like a phoenix from the ashes, client retention rates improved, and employee morale soared to new heights. The numbers spoke volumes: a 25% increase in quarterly sales and a 40% uptick in client retention. The company had weathered the storm and emerged stronger and more resilient.

Upon reflection, the Sales Director acknowledged that while their strategy was a success, it was not without its criticisms. Some naysayers had believed the focus on existing clients would divert attention from new market opportunities. However, the bolstered client relationships led to a network effect, with referrals bringing in new business organically.

Visual aids, such as growth charts and client satisfaction graphs, dotted the company's internal presentations, reinforcing the tangible success of the new strategy. It was a testament to the power of strategic sales planning.

But what does this mean for the broader narrative of strategic sales success? It illustrates that a company, regardless of size or industry, must be willing to adapt to rethink its approach in the face of adversity. It's about understanding that the sales landscape is ever-changing, and so must our strategies.

As we turn the page on this case study, consider: Is your sales team equipped to pivot with the tides of change? Are you prepared to question the status quo, to reinvent the wheel if that's what it takes to achieve next-level success?

In the grand tapestry of strategic sales planning, each thread— each decision and action—must be woven with intention and purpose. Let the rhythm of your strategies be as fluid as the markets you navigate, and may your plans carry the cadence of a wellorchestrated symphony.

Now, my dear reader, as you contemplate the essence of strategic sales success, ask yourself: What moves will you make when your back is against the wall and the game is on the line? How will you write the next chapter of your own success story?

CHAPTER 5

THE ART OF STORY SELLING

Elements of a Compelling Sales Story

In the ever-evolving landscape of commerce, the art of storytelling emerges as a beacon, guiding prospects through a journey from mere awareness to loyal patronage. As we embark on this chapter of 'Next Level Selling – Next Level Life,' we shall uncover the tapestry of techniques that constitute a compelling sales narrative. A story that does not merely speak to the mind but resonates with the heart.

As dawn heralds the day, so does our introduction to the list of key elements that form the bedrock of an engaging sales story. These elements are not mere placeholders in a narrative; they are the pulsating heartbeats of a story that lives, breathes, and inspires action.

The core threads of our story's fabric will include Relatability, Conflict and Resolution, Emotional Pull, Authenticity, Clarity and Focus, and a Strong Call to Action. Each

81

stand as a pillar, holding aloft the structure of a tale that can sway the scales in favor of your offering.

Relatability

A tale that whispers secrets of the familiar beckons your audience closer. Relatability is the bridge that connects your story to the heart of your listener. It is the mirror in which they see their reflections, their desires, challenges, and dreams. Embedding relatable characters, settings, or situations gives your audience a stake in the narrative.

Anecdotes of clients who have walked the same path faced similar obstacles, and triumphed can serve as powerful testimonials. Consider the case of Jane, a small business owner whose struggles with managing inventory were quelled by your innovative software solution. Jane's story is not unique, but it is real and relatable.

Demonstrate practical applications by highlighting how your product seamlessly integrates into your customers' daily lives. If Jane can conquer her challenges, so can your audience. This is the promise of relatability.

Conflict and Resolution

What is a story without its crescendo, the mounting tension that demands resolution? Conflict introduces the element of suspense and engages the audience's innate desire for resolution. It is the mountain peak your hero must summit, the dragon they must slay.

Dive into the heart of the problem your product solves. Be explicit about the pain points, and then, with a masterful stroke, reveal how your offering provides the much sought-after resolution. Evidence of success stories, statistics that show improvement, or case studies that detail the journey from conflict to resolution all serve as compelling reinforcements.

In practice, illustrating how your product bridged the gap for a struggling entrepreneur, turning their fortunes around, translates the abstract into reality. Conflict and resolution make the story— and your product—inescapable.

Emotional Pull

Emotions are the silent whispers that nudge us toward a decision. An emotionally charged story can be the difference between apathy and action. Infuse your narrative with your audience's joys, fears, and aspirations. Paint your story with the colors of triumph, relief, and satisfaction your product brings.

Quotes from satisfied customers, infused with genuine emotion, can elevate the credibility of your story. "I felt a weight lift off my shoulders," claims a relieved customer, encapsulating the liberation your service afforded them.

By presenting scenarios that evoke empathy or elation, you weave the emotional pull into the practical fabric of your sales story. It is not merely a product but a catalyst for positive emotional transformation.

Authenticity

In a world awash with hyperbole and embellishment, authenticity is a lighthouse, signaling truth and trust. An authentic story is grounded in reality; it is honest about the capabilities and limitations of your product. Authenticity fosters trust, which is the currency of repeat business and referrals.

Integrate authentic elements by sharing behind-the-scenes glimpses, the philosophy that drives your brand, or the meticulous care that goes into product development. Authenticity is corroborated by genuine customer feedback and the unscripted voice of experience.

In practice, authenticity means aligning the story with the true impact of your product. It is the unvarnished truth that not only tells but also shows the integrity of your brand.

Clarity and Focus

A sharp story cuts through the noise and distractions, delivering its message precisely. Clarity and focus ensure that your narrative remains on point, guiding your audience through the salient features of your offering without veering into tangents.

To achieve clarity, use simple language that conveys complex ideas without convolution. A one-line paragraph can serve as a beacon of focus: "Our software turns data into decisions." Such clarity leaves a lasting impression.

In application, clarity means that every feature and benefit of your product is presented with directness and simplicity, ensuring that the audience grasps the essence without confusion.

Strong Call to Action

Finally, the denouement of your story must be a strong call to action (CTA). A CTA is the rallying cry that spurs your audience into motion. The signpost points to the next step, the invitation to transform passive interest into active engagement.

A compelling CTA is clear, urgent, and imbued with value. "Join the ranks of successful entrepreneurs. Try our solution today." This CTA not only prompts action but also reinforces the aspirational identity of the prospect.

In the real world, a CTA is a bridge from story to reality, from potential to actuality. The crucial link turns a compelling narrative into a commercial triumph.

As we weave these elements together, each transition carries us seamlessly from one vital point to the next, crafting a narrative that is not just heard or seen but felt and remembered. This is the essence of a compelling sales story: a symphony of points that resonate in harmony to capture the imagination and compel the heart to action.

Crafting Your Personal Sales Narrative

Your ability to weave a personal sales narrative can mark the difference between mediocrity and meteoric success in a marketplace of ideas and products. This narrative isn't simply a string of well-chosen words; it is your unique fingerprint on the canvas of commerce, a story that resonates with clients and distinguishes you from the cacophony of competitors. In 'Next Level Selling - Next Level Life,' we turn the spotlight onto you, the architect of your own story, guiding you step by step to mold your experiences, values, and vision into a compelling narrative that captivates your audience.

Picture yourself at the helm of a boardroom, the focus of rapt attention as you unveil an enthralling story that your prospects can't help but see their future entwined with your offering. This is the pinnacle of sales artistry, where your narrative becomes the golden thread in the tapestry of your client's needs and desires.

The objective is crystal clear: craft a personal sales narrative that engages your clients and elevates their perception of your product or service to an indispensable life enhancer. To embark on this journey, you must blend introspection, creativity, and a keen understanding of your audience. Begin by inventorying your experiences, identifying the values defining your brand, and pinpointing your product or service's transformative impact on its users.

Let's first sketch the overarching structure of this narrative odyssey. It begins with a deep dive into your personal and brand identity, then constructing a storyline that interlaces your values with client aspirations. The climax reveals the transformative power of your offering, and the conclusion ties it all together with a compelling call to action.

Now, let us dissect this structure, examining each segment with the meticulousness of a master storyteller.

Initially, introspect on your journey—both personal and professional. What pivotal moments have shaped your approach to business? Perhaps it was an early challenge that taught you resilience or an encounter that underscored the importance of customer empathy. These are the seeds from which your narrative will grow.

Next, detail how these experiences translate into the values that underpin your brand. Do you prioritize innovation, or is your hallmark the reliability of time-tested solutions? This isn't merely about what you sell; it's about why you sell it and why it matters.

As you craft your story, remember to weave in the texture of detail. A vivid description of a challenge you faced, the emotions that surged as you navigated through it, and the triumphant solution you devised can draw your audience into the heart of your narrative. "There was a moment," you might recount, "when all seemed lost—when the very fabric of my venture hung by a thread. But it was in that crucible of challenge that our breakthrough technology was born, a technology that now ensures no entrepreneur faces that kind of uncertainty again."

Sprinkle in practical advice—nuggets of wisdom your clients can apply in their ventures. Caution them against common pitfalls: "Beware the lure of shortcuts; the path to enduring success is paved with diligence and authenticity."

To validate your narrative's resonance, seek feedback from trusted colleagues or a focus group representative of your target audience. Their reactions will be the litmus test for the effectiveness of your story. Furthermore, if you encounter skepticism or disinterest, delve into the source. Is the problem rooted in a lack of clarity or emotional connection? Troubleshooting these issues early on will strengthen the final delivery of your narrative.

As you fine-tune your story, consider each sentence and each word. Start sentences with varying structures, painting your narrative with the broad strokes of nouns, verbs' sharp outlines, and adjectives' subtle shades. For example, "Innovation ignites our passion. Tirelessly, we craft solutions that redefine industries. Our commitment: to transform your daily struggles into triumphs."

Remember to pose direct questions that invite reflection. "Have you ever faced a challenge so daunting it seemed insurmountable?" Such queries engage the listener, prompting them to project their experiences onto the canvas of your story.

Maintain simplicity in your language, choosing words for precision and impact rather than complexity. A stand-alone sentence often speaks volumes: "We changed the game."

Be mindful of rhythm, allowing the cadence of your words to ebb and flow like a melody that enchants the listener. Quotes from satisfied customers or snippets of dialogue add authenticity and variety, anchoring your narrative in reality.

And, in the tradition of 'show, don't tell,' let your story unfold through examples and anecdotes. Instead of asserting the benefits of your product, describe the day-to-day transformation experienced by a user: "John, once overwhelmed by administrative chaos, now navigates his workday with serene efficiency, thanks to our platform."

By meticulously crafting your personal sales narrative, you are not just selling a product or service but offering a piece of a dream, a chapter in your clients' journey toward success. This narrative will linger in their minds long after the boardroom empties, beckoning them toward a partnership that promises a transaction and a transformation.

Using Metaphors and Analogies

When it comes to sales, clarity is king. It is the golden key that unlocks understanding and the bridge that connects a product to a customer's needs. One potent tool in achieving this clarity is using metaphors and analogies, which can distill complex sales messages into comprehensible and relatable terms. This chapter delves into the art of employing these linguistic devices to elevate your sales pitch into an engaging narrative that resonates deeply with your clientele.

Imagine, if you will, that you are not merely a salesperson but a translator. Your clients are travelers in a foreign land, and your product is a map written in an unfamiliar script. Metaphors and analogies become the lexicon through which you translate this script into a language that sings meaningfully and purposefully. They are the lenses that bring into focus the blurred lines of technical jargon and abstract concepts.

To fully grasp the power of these tools, let us first explore their essence. A metaphor is a figure of speech that describes an object or action in a way that isn't true but helps explain an idea or make a comparison. Conversely, an analogy is a comparison between two things, typically for explanation or clarification. They are the threads that weave the fabric of understanding, connecting the unfamiliar to the familiar.

Consider the example of a cloud-based data storage service. To a technologically savvy audience, the intricacies of cloud computing might be as clear as daylight. But what of those to whom this is uncharted territory? You might say, "Think of cloud storage as a bank vault where your digital valuables—photos, documents, music—are kept safe. You can deposit or withdraw them from anywhere without carrying them around." Instantly, a complex service is likened to a daily, understandable activity.

Let's shift our gaze to another illustration: the sales process itself. Picture it as a journey. You, the salesperson, are the seasoned guide, and your client, the eager yet inexperienced traveler. Your product is the destination—a place of fulfillment and solutions. Along the way, you encounter obstacles but equipped with the right tools and knowledge, you help the traveler navigate through. The metaphor simplifies the process and adds an emotional layer that can strengthen the bond between you and your client.

Now, what if we viewed these concepts from a different angle?

While a metaphor is a direct substitution, an analogy is more like a bridge. If you're introducing a revolutionary new product, you might draw an analogy to the advent of smartphones. "Just as smartphones redefined communication by converging multiple devices into one, our product amalgamates all your needs into a single, seamless solution."

Incorporating data and facts into these narratives can heighten their impact. For instance, when you present statistics about the increased efficiency users experience with your service, it's not merely a number—it's a reflection of the hours saved, akin to gaining an extra day each week. This contextualization transforms dry data into a vivid image of extra leisure or productivity.

While folding complex terms into our narrative, we must act like we're peeling an artichoke, revealing the heart beneath the layers. Take 'synchronization across devices,' a term that can baffle the uninitiated. Break it down: "It's like having a team of messengers, ensuring that no matter where you are, your information is always up-to-date and at your fingertips."

As we draw this chapter close, let us crystallize the essence of using metaphors and analogies in sales. They are the storytellers' magic, transforming abstract concepts into tangible experiences and complex ideas into simple truths. They are not mere ornaments of language but foundational pillars that uphold the temple of understanding.

Remember, the next time you find yourself in the labyrinth of a sales pitch, let metaphors and analogies be your Ariadne's thread, guiding you and your clients to the clarity that awaits at the journey's end. With these tools in your arsenal, elevate your selling to an art and your clients' lives to the next level.

Storytelling Techniques for Different Audiences

The art of storytelling emerges as a beacon of connection, bridging the chasm between a product's features and a customer's needs. A compelling narrative can enchant and persuade, transforming the mundane into the extraordinary. Yet, to truly harness the power of storytelling, one must become a chameleon, adapting tales to the vivid hues of different customer profiles.

Consider the entrepreneur and the retiree—two distinct individuals on disparate paths. The entrepreneur, driven by ambition and innovation, thrives on risk and potential. On the other hand, the retiree seeks comfort and security, having weathered the storms of a lifelong career. Herein lies the purpose of our comparison: to unveil how a singular storytelling approach can be tailored to resonate with each, magnifying the allure of our offering.

The criteria for our analysis are simple yet demanding understanding the audience's values, desires, and experiences. For the entrepreneur, the story of a product must pulse with opportunity and growth, hinting at uncharted territories awaiting their conquest. In contrast, the narrative for the retiree should evoke a tapestry of reliability and ease, a solution that promises a serene continuation of their well-earned peace.

Let us delve into the similarities of these stories. Both audiences seek value and assurance that their choice is prudent and beneficial. The entrepreneur and retiree wish to be protagonists in a tale that succeeds, whether financial triumph or tranquil enjoyment. Here, storytelling shares a common thread— the promise of a product enhancing life's narrative.

Yet, as we shift our gaze to the contrasts, the subtleties of storytelling begin to shimmer. For the entrepreneur, we spin a yarn of innovation; our product is the key to unlocking new markets and catapulting their business forward. We speak of scalability; of the edge they'll hold in a competitive arena. The dialogue is peppered with terms like 'cutting-edge', 'disruptive', and 'game-changing'.

Conversely, the retiree's story is swathed in the comfort of familiarity, a quilt woven from threads of trust and simplicity. Our product is a steadfast companion in their journey, a reliable beacon amidst the fog of modern complexities. We use language that soothes and reassures—'proven,' 'stable,' and 'user-friendly.'

Imagine, if you will, a visual aid—a diagram, perhaps. On one axis, we plot the entrepreneur's desire for growth against the retiree's longing for stability. On the other, we trace their shared need for value. The resulting graph is not merely a collection of lines and data points; it is a storyteller's map, guiding us through the terrain of human desires.

From this analysis emerges a profound insight: while the core of our story remains constant—the promise of a life enhanced by our product—the hues and shades we use to color it must shift according to the audience. To the entrepreneur, our product is a vessel sailing toward a horizon of prosperity. To the retiree, it is a familiar, secure and inviting cottage amidst the wilderness of change.

The relevance of our comparison to the contemporary world of sales cannot be overstated. In an age where personalization reigns supreme, understanding the unique heartbeat of each customer segment is not just beneficial; it is essential.

Let us pose a direct question: How does one ensure that their story speaks to the audience and sings to their soul? The answer is both simple and complex. One must listen intently to the whispers of their customers' dreams and fears, weaving narratives that mirror their inner landscapes.

In crafting these tales, we must be judicious with our language, choosing words with the precision of a poet. A single, well-placed line can illuminate a feature, making it a beacon of desirability. "This software does not just streamline your operations; it turns time into your loyal ally, stretching minutes into moments of creation."

To wrap our musings in the cloak of practicality, let us not forget the power of the anecdote. A story of an entrepreneur who shattered barriers with our product or a retiree who rediscovered leisure can be more convincing than the most eloquent of feature lists.

In conclusion, storytelling in sales is not a one-size-fits-all garment. It is a bespoke suit tailored to the contours of each customer's life. As storytellers, our task is to fashion these garments with care and intention, dressing our products in narratives that resonate with the aspirations of every individual. In doing so, we elevate their experience, and indeed, their life, to the next level.

The Role of Emotion in Story Selling

The role of emotion in story selling cannot be overstated. It is the heartbeat of a narrative, the undercurrent that sweeps the buyer along a journey from skepticism to trust, from interest to action. But what about emotion, which gives it such persuasive power in the sales process?

At its core, emotion is the psychological experience associated with mood, temperament, personality, and disposition. It colors our perceptions and guides our decisions, often operating beneath the surface of our conscious awareness. Emotional connections in sales hinge on the ability to align a product's story with the feelings and emotional desires of the customer.

Empathy, authenticity, and relevance are key elements of emotional engagement in story selling. Empathy allows the seller to enter the buyer's shoes, understanding their desires and pain points.

Authenticity ensures that the story being told resonates as true and credible. Relevance ties the story to the buyer's immediate needs and aspirations, making it feel personal and bespoke.

Though the concept of emotional selling seems modern, its roots stretch back through the annals of history. The ancient bazaars teemed with merchants who knew the power of a personal connection. At the same time, the traveling salesmen of yesteryear were masters at reading their audience and delivering tales that tugged at the heartstrings.

Positioning emotion within the broader sales framework becomes the linchpin of customer engagement. It bridges the gap between a product's features and the customer's emotional response, turning abstract benefits into tangible experiences. For example, a real estate agent doesn't merely sell houses; they sell homes and nesting places for memories and dreams. The agent's ability to evoke feelings of comfort, security, and belonging can decide a sale.

Real-world applications of emotional story selling abound. Consider the car salesperson who doesn't just highlight a vehicle's horsepower but speaks to the thrill of the open road and the freedom it represents. Or the software vendor who doesn't only discuss technical specifications but addresses the peace of mind that comes with efficient, secure data management.

A common misconception is that emotional story selling is manipulative or deceitful. On the contrary, when done with integrity, it is about finding and highlighting the genuine emotional value that a product or service can bring to a customer's life. It is not about creating false stories but about bringing real benefits into sharper emotional focus.

Now, let us ponder this: What happens when a story is so compelling that it stops being just a story and starts feeling like a shared experience? This is the transformative power of emotion in sales. A well-told story, imbued with the right emotional cues, can elevate a simple transaction into a meaningful exchange.

Strong verbs and nouns carry the weight of this narrative. A tech gadget doesn't 'help' one keep organized; it 'ensures' one's day flows seamlessly. A fitness program doesn't simply 'offer' health benefits; it 'promises' rejuvenation and vitality.

Within the span of a single breath, consider the potency of a one-line paragraph: Emotion is the silent language of connection.

Simple language serves as the vessel for delivering complex emotional payloads. It is not about dumbing down the message but about refining it to its essence so its impact can be felt immediately and deeply.

A story's rhythm and cadence are as crucial as its content. A staccato burst of short sentences can build excitement, while a longer, flowing sentence can soothe and reassure. The tempo of the narrative must match the mood of the moment.

Quotations or dialogues add flesh to the bones of a story, making it relive in the customer's mind. "When I first tried this product," a satisfied customer might say, "I felt like I was finally in control of my day."

And finally, the golden rule of 'show, don't tell' ensures the story is heard and felt. Instead of asserting that a product is reliable, a story can illustrate how it has never failed, even in the most demanding of circumstances.

In weaving together these threads of storytelling, emotion stands as the vibrant dye that gives color to the tapestry. It turns features into benefits, benefits into experiences, and experiences into memories. And in the memory of a well-told story, laced with resonant emotion, lies the potential for a sale and a lifelong customer.

Visual Storytelling in Sales Presentations

Visual storytelling has emerged as a compelling force in the realm of sales presentations, capable of captivating an audience and cementing your message in their memories. When you master the art of visual storytelling, you don't just deliver data; you weave a narrative tapestry that can transport your prospects to the next level of engagement. This chapter is a deep dive into how you can harness the power of visuals to tell a story, inspire action, and foster a life-changing connection with your clients.

Imagine for a moment that you are not just a salesperson but a director of a movie where every slide is a scene, every chart a character, and every image a chance to touch the heart and mind of your viewer. Your objective? To lead your audience through a journey that culminates in the realization that they need what you're offering to improve their own story—their life or business.

You'll need a few tools to embark on this journey: compelling images, a storytelling mindset, an understanding of your audience, and the technology to bring your visuals to life. These are the prerequisites to crafting a visual story that informs and transforms.

Let's begin with a broad overview of the visual storytelling process in sales presentations. This journey encompasses understanding your audience, crafting a narrative, selecting powerful images and graphics, and tying them all together with the thread of your spoken words.

Dive deeper, and you'll see that each step is critical. First, know your audience—what resonates with them, their pain points, and what they dream of achieving. Next, define the narrative arc of your presentation, ensuring it has a beginning that hooks, a middle that builds, and an end that calls to action. Selecting visuals is not about filling space but choosing images that evoke the right emotions and underscore your message. Integrate charts and graphs to display data and tell a story of change, contrast, or progress.

A few tips can elevate your visual storytelling. Always align visuals with the spoken word for a seamless narrative experience. Use high-quality images to avoid distractions and maintain professionalism. Remember, less is more—avoid clutter and let each visual breathe.

To validate the effectiveness of your presentation, seek feedback. Conduct a dry run with colleagues or clients who can provide honest critiques. Did the visuals make the story clearer? Did they evoke the intended emotions? The answers will guide your refinement.

If you face obstacles like a lack of engagement or misunderstanding of the message, troubleshoot by revisiting your narrative flow and visual choices. Ensure each visual serves a purpose and reinforces your key points.

Now, let's bring this story to life. Picture a room full of potential clients, their attention fixed on the screen behind you. With every slide, you're not just presenting features and benefits but taking them on a journey. A graph morphs from flat lines to a mountain range, representing growth. A series of photographs transition from monochrome to vibrant color, symbolizing solution and success. Your words anchor these visuals, guiding your audience through your proposed transformation.

Consider this: What if your presentation isn't just informative but unforgettable? What if it's not a monologue but a dialogue where every image invites your audience to imagine the next chapter of their success story?

In this chapter, you've been given a palette and a canvas. It's time to paint not just a picture but a future. As the adage goes, a picture is worth a thousand words. In sales, the right picture paired with the right words can be worth infinitely more.

Visual storytelling in sales presentations isn't just about selling a product or service; it's about offering a pathway to an aspirational life. It's about showing your clients not just what is but what could be. It's about turning the ordinary into the extraordinary, one slide at a time.

As you close your presentation, leave them with a lasting image that encapsulates your message—a beacon that continues to glow long after the lights in the meeting room have dimmed. This is the essence of next-level selling: creating a next-level life for your clients through the art of visual storytelling.

Analyzing Successful Sales Stories

The stories that resonate most are those of triumph and transformation—tales that inform and inspire. As we delve into the anatomy of a successful sales story, it's crucial to recognize that the victories achieved are not solely about the numbers; they embody the broader implications of what it means to excel in the art of selling truly. This exploration is a journey into the heart of such a story, offering a blueprint for replicating success.

Our case study unfolds against the backdrop of a fiercely competitive technology market. The industry, known for its rapid pace and cutthroat rivalry, sets the stage for a narrative rife with challenges and ripe for strategic conquests.

The main players in this saga are a burgeoning tech startup and a seasoned sales team led by an astute sales director, Alex Mercer. With a blend of fresh talent and experienced professionals, the team was as diverse as it was ambitious. Their product, an innovative cloud storage solution, promised unparalleled security and efficiency, but breaking into the market dominated by established giants was a Herculean task.

The central challenge was how to penetrate a saturated market and capture the attention of enterprises that were deeply entrenched with competitors. The startup's unique selling proposition was clear, but the path to convincing potential clients to make the switch was fraught with obstacles.

The approach was multifaceted, combining meticulous research, personalized outreach, and a bold value proposition. Alex and his team began by diving deep into understanding their prospective clients' pain points, gathering intelligence that would later be the cornerstone of their sales strategy. They crafted tailored narratives that spoke directly to the concerns and aspirations of each potential customer, positioning their cloud solution not just as a product but as a strategic partner in the client's growth.

As the results started pouring in, the numbers told a compelling story. The startup secured several high-profile contracts, outperforming its targets by a remarkable margin. Market share grew, investor confidence soared, and the industry began noticing. The sales team's strategy had not only worked; it had catapulted them into the limelight.

Upon reflection, the success of this venture could be dissected into key elements: a deep understanding of the client's needs, a sales narrative that was both compelling and personal, and the relentless pursuit of excellence. However, amidst the celebration, there was room for critique. Some argued that the aggressive growth strategy could be unsustainable in the long run. Others questioned the scalability of such a hands-on, customized approach.

Visual aids played a significant role in this story. Complex data was distilled into clear, engaging infographics that captured the essence of the startup's value. Charts showed the upward trajectory of client acquisition and retention, while diagrams illustrated the robustness of the cloud solution's architecture.

But what does this success mean in the grander scheme of things? It exemplifies the quintessential elements of next-level selling—empathy, customization, and unwavering determination. When executed with precision and passion, these tenets are not just effective; they're transformative.

Let's pause for a moment. Imagine you're in Alex's shoes, facing an impenetrable market. What strategies would you employ? How would you differentiate your offering in a sea of sameness?

While unique in its details, this story is universal in its theme. It serves as a testament to the power of strategic salesmanship and its impact on a business's trajectory. It's a reminder that at the very core of selling, beyond the tactics and the techniques, lies the profound ability to connect and to solve—to elevate a customer's experience from the ordinary to the extraordinary.

As we move forward, let's carry with us the lessons learned from this case study. Let's aspire not only to meet targets but to exceed them in ways that leave a lasting mark on our clients and our industry. In the pursuit of next-level selling lies the potential for a next-level life—a life characterized by growth, fulfillment, and the unending quest for excellence.

The next chapter will explore how sales professionals can maintain momentum and avoid complacency following significant wins. After all, the journey doesn't end with a single success story. It's an ongoing saga of evolution and reinvention. What will be your next chapter?

CHAPTER 6

BELIEF SYSTEMS AND SALES BEHAVIORS

Identifying Limiting Beliefs

I n the bustling landscape of contemporary commerce, where the clatter of keystrokes and the hum of digital transactions punctuate the air, a silent adversary often lurks in the shadows.

This elusive and deeply rooted foe can sabotage even the most skilled sales professionals, hindering their ascent toward peak performance. The insidious presence of limiting beliefs—those stealthy whispers of self-doubt and assumed inabilities-constrain. one's potential.

Consider Sarah, a seasoned saleswoman who, despite her experience, finds herself consistently falling short of her targets. She possesses the skills, the knowledge, and the drive, yet an invisible barrier seems to repel her from the success she so ardently chases. Like many others in her field, Sarah has yet to recognize that the primary obstacle she faces is nestled within her convictions.

The problem, stark and unyielding, lies in the heart of one's psyche. The collection of limiting beliefs whispers tales of inadequacy into the eager ears of ambition. "You're not good enough," they say, or "You can't handle rejection," and the deadliest of all, "This is as good as it gets." These beliefs, once internalized, manifest as self-fulfilling prophecies, shackling salespeople to a plateau of mediocrity.

If left unchecked, the consequences are dire. A salesperson weighed down by limiting beliefs may experience plummeting performance, declining morale, and, ultimately, a career that slowly spirals into obsolescence. The ripple effects extend beyond the individual—teams suffer, businesses falter, and the vibrant dance of commerce stumbles.

Yet, there is hope—a beacon in the fog of doubt. The solution lies in the deliberate excavation and dismantling of these limiting beliefs. It begins with cultivating self-awareness and a steadfast commitment to personal growth.

The first step in this transformative journey is to identify the limiting beliefs that reside in the undercurrent of one's thoughts. To do this, one must observe one's mind, questioning the veracity of each negative belief. "Is it true that I am not cut out for success?" "Have I truly explored all avenues of growth?" Such introspection can illuminate the hidden corners of one's belief system.

Once these beliefs are brought to light, the process of reframing can commence. This involves challenging the old, restrictive narratives and replacing them with empowering alternatives. For instance, instead of succumbing to the belief that rejection is a mark of failure, one can choose to see it as an opportunity for learning and refinement.

Implementing this solution requires discipline and persistence. It is a practice of mental reconditioning that involves daily affirmations, mindfulness exercises, and the pursuit of knowledge to reinforce one's new, empowering beliefs. Each sales call, each presentation, and each negotiation become an arena to strengthen this new mindset.

Evidence of implementing such practices abounds. Take the case of James, a once-underperforming sales executive whose turnaround story is a testament to the power of belief. By identifying and restructuring his limiting beliefs, James saw a 30% increase in sales within mere months. His newfound confidence radiated, attracting clients and opportunities like never before.

While this method is potent, alternative solutions do exist. Some individuals may find solace and success through mentorship, where the guidance and encouragement of a seasoned professional can help dispel limiting beliefs. Others may opt for more structured cognitive-behavioral approaches, working with a therapist or coach to systematically deconstruct and rebuild their belief systems.

In the panorama of sales, where every handshake, every pitch, and every close is a brushstroke on the canvas of one's career, the power of belief cannot be overstated. Ultimately, it is not solely the product one sells nor the strategy one employs but the deep-seated convictions that drive the relentless pursuit of excellence.

One must ask oneself: What beliefs are guiding my actions? Are they serving my ascent, or have they anchored me to the ground?

Identifying and overcoming limiting beliefs is not merely an exercise in self-improvement; it is the gateway to a next-level life, both personally and professionally. When the chains of doubt are broken, a salesperson is unbounded, capable of reaching heights previously unimagined. It is a journey that begins with a single, yet profound, step—recognizing the invisible barriers we have unwittingly erected around ourselves.

So, take a moment, reflect on the words etched across these pages, and ask yourself: What's stopping me from achieving my next level? The answer may be the key to unlocking a life of limitless potential.

Fostering Positive Sales Beliefs

As we voyage further into the heart of 'Next Level Selling - Next Level Life,' we arrive at a vista where our beliefs are not barriers but bridges to our success. Imagine standing at the precipice of possibility, poised to cross into a realm where each belief nurtures your sales prowess and catalyzes your growth. Welcome to the chapter on "Fostering Positive Sales Beliefs."

Establish the Goal:

In this exploration, we aim to cultivate a garden of beliefs that will empower your sales effectiveness. Like a gardener who nurtures plants, you will learn to tend to your beliefs, ensuring they are positive, robust, and conducive to personal and professional growth. By the end of this journey, you will possess a belief system that propels you towards your sales targets with unwavering conviction.

Necessary Materials or Prerequisites:

To embark on this transformative odyssey, you need a willingness to introspect, an openness to change, and a commitment to action. You'll require tools such as a journal for reflection, access to motivational resources, and a network of supportive peers or mentors. Most importantly, you'll need resilience, for the path to altering deep-seated beliefs is often strewn with challenges.

Begin with a Broad Overview:

The roadmap before you will unfold in stages: awareness, excavation, construction, and maintenance. Initially, you'll become aware of the current landscape of your beliefs. Then, you'll dig deep to unearth those that are limiting. With a clean slate, you'll construct new, empowering beliefs. Finally, you'll learn to maintain and reinforce these beliefs to ensure they remain strong against the winds of adversity.

Dive into the Detailed Steps:

Awareness is the dawn of change. Start by identifying the beliefs that currently guide your sales behaviors. Which convictions serve you, and which sabotage you? Recognize patterns in your thinking, especially after setbacks or challenges. What stories are you telling yourself?

Next, excavate these beliefs. Like artifacts of the mind, they must be delicately unearthed and examined. Challenge each one: Is this belief rooted in fact, or is it an outdated script from past experiences?

Now, construct new beliefs. Sculpt them with the clay of positivity and the water of truth. "I am a capable salesperson," you might affirm, "and with each interaction, I grow and improve." These declarations become the building blocks of your renewed mindset.

Maintenance is about cultivation. Regularly affirm your new beliefs. Nurture them through continued learning, seeking out success stories, and surrounding yourself with those who uplift you. Remember, a belief is only as strong as your attention.

Some Tips and Warnings:

Be vigilant. Old beliefs may resurface, disguised in new forms. When they do, confront them with evidence of your progress.

Beware of becoming complacent; the garden of your mind requires constant tending.

Testing or Validation:

You will know you've successfully fostered positive sales beliefs when you observe a shift in your behaviors and outcomes. Track your sales metrics, note the ease with which you handle rejection, and watch for an overall increase in your sales performance.

If you find yourself reverting to old patterns, do not despair. Troubleshooting these moments is part of the process. Reflect on what triggered the relapse and reaffirm your commitment to your new beliefs. Seek guidance from mentors or colleagues who can provide an objective perspective.

In the realm of selling, the power of belief is the silent engine driving every action. As you rewrite the narrative of your sales career, remember that every thought shapes your reality. Choose beliefs that lift you higher and watch as your sales and life ascend to unprecedented levels.

Pause for a moment. Can you feel the burgeoning strength of your new convictions? Are they not the wings upon which your sales success will soar? Embrace them, and step boldly into your next-level life.

Aligning Beliefs With Sales Goals

In the competitive sales arena, where every handshake and smile can tip the scales, aligning beliefs with sales goals isn't just a strategy; it's the bedrock of success. The landscape of sales is ever-changing, but the psychological foundations remain steadfast. As we delve into the complexities of aligning beliefs with sales goals, it's vital to understand that this alignment is the compass guiding sales professionals to their North Star - the realization of their life's work not only in their careers but also in their personal lives.

Envision a sales professional, Jack, whose eyes gleam with the promise of achievement. He's a mosaic of ambition, yet his results are a mere shadow of his potential. The root of the issue? His beliefs are out of sync with his objectives. Jack's belief that he's not a natural at sales is a chain around his potential, anchoring him to mediocrity. This illustrates the crux of the matter: when beliefs are misaligned with goals, it's akin to rowing against the tide.

What awaits Jack and any sales professional in his shoes if this misalignment persists? The consequences are manifold. For starters, a stagnation in career progression looms large, casting a shadow over future aspirations. Moreover, there's a risk of a cascading loss of confidence, which can bleed into personal wellbeing, tarnishing the luster of one's life both within and outside the office walls.

But there's hope on the horizon. The antidote to this malaise is a realignment of beliefs that can turn the tide in Jack's favor. The solution is both simple and complex: instill beliefs that resonate with the drumbeat of his goals. This is not about hollow affirmations or wishful thinking; it's about cultivating a mindset that is congruent with the outcomes he seeks.

The first step in this transformative process is self-reflection. Jack must excavate his current belief system and identify beliefs contradicting his sales goals. He needs to ask himself tough questions. What are the stories he's been telling himself about his sales ability? Are they tales of caution or chronicles of conquest? It's a time for honesty, to strip away the veneer and confront the beliefs that are holding him back.

Next, Jack must craft a new set of beliefs that act as pillars supporting his aspirations. This involves a careful selection of empowering thoughts and convictions. He must believe that he is capable of achieving his sales targets and that each setback is a steppingstone to greater success. This shift in mindset is akin to planting a garden of possibility in the fertile soil of his consciousness.

Implementation of this new belief system is a daily endeavor. Jack must integrate his new beliefs into every facet of his sales strategy. This could mean starting each day with a visualization of success or systematically challenging negative thoughts when they arise with evidence of his past successes. It's about reinforcing the new beliefs until they are as robust as the old ones once were.

Evidence of this approach can be found in the annals of sales history. Countless sales professionals have testified to the power of belief alignment, citing improved performance, increased resilience, and a newfound zest for the sales process. These stories are not mere anecdotes but testaments to the transformative power of belief.

Some may argue that other solutions, such as focusing solely on skill development or adopting aggressive sales tactics, could suffice. While these approaches have their merits, they are akin to treating the symptoms rather than the disease. Without the foundation of aligned beliefs, any improvement will likely be short-lived.

Let's not mince words: the path to realigning beliefs with sales goals is not a stroll in the park. It demands introspection, a willingness to confront uncomfortable truths, and the tenacity to forge new mental pathways. But the rewards are manifold, echoing in the halls of professional triumph and whispering in the quiet moments of personal reflection.

Imagine Jack, weeks later, standing before his sales team, sharing his journey of realignment. His words are a tapestry of conviction, woven with threads of struggle and triumph. His story is a beacon of hope, illuminating the path for others to follow.

Sales professionals who dare to embark on this journey of belief alignment are not just selling products or services but selling themselves on the vision of what they can become. They are architects of their destiny, sculpting their reality with the chisel of aligned beliefs. This is the essence of 'Next Level Selling - Next Level Life.'

So, as you turn the page on this chapter, pose yourself this direct question: what beliefs are you holding that don't serve your sales goals? And are you ready to replace them with convictions that will elevate you to the next level of your selling journey and, in turn, your life? The answer lies within, waiting to be uncovered and embraced.

Behavior Modification Techniques

Pursuing excellence in sales is akin to embarking on a quest for personal mastery; each strategy honed, each skill refined, propels one closer to their zenith. The journey, however, is laden with the need for constant adaptation and growth, with behavior modification standing as a crucial pivot upon which the scales of success are tipped. In this chapter, we will navigate the labyrinth of behavior modification, a path that promises to lead to the pinnacle of sales effectiveness and a vibrant, fulfilling life.

Let us first solidify our objective. The goal that we aim to accomplish is straightforward yet profound: to adopt new behaviors that align with successful sales outcomes. This transformation is not merely about altering surface-level actions; it's a metamorphosis of the patterns that dictate our daily sales endeavors.

Before we commence, we must list the necessary materials or prerequisites. You will require an unwavering commitment to self-improvement, a reflective and open mindset, and a readiness to implement change. Recording tools such as a journal or digital app for tracking progress and a supportive network for feedback and encouragement will also be invaluable assets on this journey.

Embarking on this voyage, we look upon a broad overview of the steps that await us. To begin with, we'll identify the behaviors that need alteration. Following this, we'll delve into adopting new, beneficial behaviors. We'll then establish a system for reinforcing these behaviors and measure our progress to ensure we remain steadfast on our path.

Let's dive into the detailed steps, where the essence of our quest truly unfolds. The first step is to identify the behaviors that impede our sales success meticulously. Are you hesitating when it comes to cold calling? Perhaps you're not following up with prospects as diligently as you could. Scrutinize your daily routines and interactions with a critical yet compassionate eye.

Once these behaviors are laid bare, we must replace them with more productive habits. For example, if procrastination is your nemesis, you could tackle the most challenging tasks first thing in the morning. If reluctance to engage with clients is the issue, commit to initiating a certain number of meaningful conversations each day.

The subsequent phase is the reinforcement of these new behaviors. This can be achieved by establishing rewards for incremental successes and by weaving the new behaviors into the fabric of your daily life until they become second nature.

In our endeavor, practical advice is a beacon that guides us through the shadows of doubt. Visualize the successful outcomes of your new behaviors, and let this vision be your lodestar. Surround yourself with affirmations that bolster your belief in your ability to change. And remember, consistency is the crucible in which behavioral transformation is forged.

As we progress, testing or validation of our new behaviors is crucial. Measure your success by setting specific, quantifiable goals. Perhaps it's increasing your sales by a certain percentage or expanding your client base by a definite number. Witnessing tangible results will be the litmus test of your commitment to behavior modification.

Should you encounter setbacks, which is an inevitable part of any transformative process, troubleshooting becomes essential. If a new behavior is not yielding the expected results, reassess and adjust your approach. Seek feedback from mentors or peers and be willing to refine your strategy.

Let's crystallize these steps with vivid imagery. Picture a seasoned archer, seamlessly drawing her bow, her form perfected through countless hours of repetition. You are that archer, and each modified behavior is an arrow, meticulously crafted and loosed towards the target of sales excellence.

Now, imagine the sense of empowerment that comes with mastering your behaviors. Can you envision yourself standing tall, a beacon of sales prowess, your every action echoing purposefully and precisely?

Consider this direct question: What behaviors currently hold you back, and are you ready to transform them into steppingstones for your ascent?

In conclusion, this chapter is not merely a collection of words but a call to action—a blueprint for those willing to sculpt their destiny with the chisel of behavior modification. The road ahead is paved with the promise of triumphs and the certainty of challenges. Yet, with each step forward, with each behavior mastered, you come closer to embodying the essence of 'Next Level Selling - Next Level Life.' Embrace the journey, for it is in this pursuit of excellence that a truly remarkable life unfolds.

The Impact of Body Language

Words are often lauded as the primary conveyors of influence. However, the silent symphony of non-verbal cues and the eloquent dance of body language wields an equally potent sway in the theater of sales interactions. This chapter delves into the nuanced world of body language and its profound impact on selling. It guides you to harness this silent language and transform it into a vibrant tool for success.

Imagine walking into a room, the air thick with anticipation. Your upright and confident posture precedes you, speaking volumes before a single word is uttered. This is the power of presence, the initial brushstroke on the canvas of perception. Body language serves as both a mirror and a window, reflecting our inner states and offering glimpses into the thoughts and feelings of others.

To understand this concept in its entirety, consider the example of a handshake. A firm grip accompanied by steady eye contact can project assurance and warmth. Conversely, a limp handshake with averted eyes might communicate disinterest or lack of confidence. In sales, such first impressions can significantly influence the trajectory of a client relationship.

Let's explore further with illustrations from the field. Picture a sales professional, Jane, who employs open gestures and a genuine smile and maintains appropriate eye contact during her pitch. Her body language exudes enthusiasm and sincerity, engendering trust and receptivity in her potential clients. On the flip side, consider John, whose crossed arms and frequent glances at the clock suggest impatience and disengagement, potentially undermining his efforts to connect with his audience.

From different perspectives, it's clear that body language can be a double-edged sword. While it has the power to build bridges, it can also erect barriers. A salesperson who is aware of their non-verbal cues and adept at reading those of their clients can navigate these waters with finesse, adjusting their approach to align with the situation.

Supporting this exploration with data, studies have shown that non-verbal communication bears a significant portion of the message in any interaction. Dr. Albert Mehrabian's research indicated that 55% of communication is through body language, 38% through tone of voice, and a mere 7% through words alone. These statistics underscore the gravity of non-verbal signals in the sales process.

Now, let's clarify some complex terms. "Mirroring" is a technique wherein the salesperson subtly copies the body language of their client. This can create a sense of rapport and familiarity but must be done delicately to avoid appearing contrived. Another term is "proxemics," which refers to the study of personal space. In sales, respecting and adjusting to a client's physical space can make a substantial difference in their comfort level.

As we draw this chapter close, let's crystallize the key takeaways. The silent language of the body speaks volumes in sales. A firm handshake, an open posture, and a warm, genuine smile can open doors and build trust. Being cognizant of and responsive to a client's body language can provide invaluable insights into their mindset and facilitate better communication.

How often do you consciously consider your body language during sales interactions? Could adjusting your non-verbal communication be the key to reaching the next level in your sales career?

Mastering the art of body language is akin to a musician finetuning their instrument, each adjustment bringing forth a more precise, resonant note. In the symphony of sales, let your body language resonate with clarity and purpose, harmonizing with your words to compose a compelling narrative of trust, confidence, and success. Remember, in the pursuit of 'Next Level Selling - Next Level Life,' it's not just what you say but how you say it—without saying anything at all.

From Belief to Behavior: Real Sales Transformations

As the dawn's early light crept through the blinds of a modest office in the heart of Chicago, the silhouette of a man could be seen leaning over a desk littered with sales charts and client files. Meet Tom, a seasoned sales veteran whose once fiery passion had dwindled to a mere flicker after years of routine pitches and unmet targets. His eyes, however, held a story yet to be told—a testament to the resilience that had carried him through countless rejections and near-wins.

Tom's journey in sales had been a roller coaster of highs and lows. He had seen days when the phone wouldn't stop ringing with eager clients and others when the silence was deafening. His belief in his ability to sell had been unshakeable—at least, that's what he had thought.

But a chance encounter at a sales conference reignited a spark within Tom. A speaker, much like myself, I stood before the crowd, speaking not of tactics and techniques but of the transformational power of belief and behavior. "Your belief," I proclaimed, "Is the compass that guides your actions, and your actions are the map to your destination." Tom's heart raced as the words resonated within him, stirring something deep inside.

Why, he wondered, had his beliefs not translated into the success he yearned for? The answer lay hidden in the depths of his daily conduct. It was not enough to believe; one must act aligned with that belief.

In the following weeks, Tom embarked on an unexpected journey of self-discovery. He examined his behaviors closely, discerning patterns that neither reflected his beliefs nor served his goals. He adopted a new mantra: "Belief inspires action, action creates habits, and habits forge destiny."

He started each day with affirmations, visualizing successful client interactions and seeing himself as the confident, persuasive salesperson he aspired to be. He replaced his routine follow-up calls with personalized, thoughtful conversations. He read voraciously, soaking up knowledge of human psychology and effective communication.

Was it possible, he pondered, to transform his sales techniques and his entire life?

The answer came in the form of a record-breaking quarter. Tom had not only met his sales targets but exceeded them with a margin that left his colleagues in awe. But it wasn't the numbers that told the real story—it was the shift in Tom's demeanor, the renewed vibrancy in his voice, and the way clients gravitated toward him.

And so, Tom's story is a testament to the universal truth that underpins this book: genuine transformation begins within. By changing his beliefs about what was possible and aligning his behaviors to match, Tom had unlocked a level of success he had previously thought unattainable.

What insights, then, can you glean from Tom's tale? How might your beliefs be shaping—or misshaping—your reality?

Imagine the possibilities if you dared to challenge the self-imposed limits of your sales career. Picture a life where each day is not a repetition of the last but a step towards a grander vision of success and fulfillment.

Let Tom's story be your gateway to understanding that the power of belief paired with deliberate action is the cornerstone of all achievement in the realm of sales and life. As you turn the pages of this book, prepare to dive deep into the experiences of those who have walked the path from belief to behavior, emerging victorious in their personal and professional lives.

Remember, in every anecdote lies a piece of wisdom waiting to be discovered, a strategy to be employed, a life to be transformed. So I ask you, what beliefs are you holding onto that no longer serve you? What behaviors are you ready to change to create your next level of success?

In the following chapters, we will explore these questions and more, providing you with the tools to sell and live at the next level. Because when you master the art of transforming belief into behavior, the possibilities are limitless.

Welcome to your journey from belief to behavior.

Belief Vs. Behavior: A Sales Dilemma

In the world of sales, two forces intertwine to shape the destiny of every salesperson—belief and behavior. The former is a deeply held conviction about one's abilities and the product's value, and the latter is the tangible actions taken to bring that conviction to life. Together, they form the bedrock of a successful career. But what happens when they are at odds? When does the belief in one's heart not mirror the behavior in one's conduct? This is the sales dilemma we are now delving into.

To understand this conundrum, we must first recognize the immense power of belief. The engine propels us forward, the inner voice whispering, "You can do this." Yet, belief without corresponding behavior is akin to a car without fuel—full of potential but stationary. Conversely, behavior without belief is a rudderless ship—motion without direction.

Why compare these two? The reason is simple: to unearth the intricate dance between the internal and the external. To unravel how a salesperson's inner world of convictions and the outer world of actions are inextricably linked. We endeavor to reveal how this dance can lead to a harmony of success or discord of disarray.

As we set the benchmarks for our analysis, we consider sales outcomes, client relationships, and personal fulfillment. These criteria serve as the lenses through which we view the interplay of belief and behavior.

Let us then examine the similarities. Both belief and behavior are under the control of the individual. They are choices that can be cultivated and refined. A salesperson who believes in the value they bring to the customer is likelier to engage in behaviors that demonstrate this value—thoroughly understanding the client's needs, presenting solutions confidently, and following up diligently.

Contrast this with the salesperson whose belief is strong but whose behavior does not align. They may possess an unwavering conviction in their product but fail to act on it, perhaps due to fear of rejection or a lack of discipline. On the other side of the spectrum lies the salesperson who behaves in all the right ways, ticking off the boxes of 'effective sales behavior,' yet lacks genuine belief in what they are selling. The result often lacks authenticity, and clients can sense it.

To elucidate these points, imagine a graph with belief on the vertical axis and behavior on the horizontal. Where they intersect, we find the sweet spot of sales success. However, when they do not align, the graph tells a story of missed opportunities and unrealized potential.

In analyzing these comparisons, we uncover broader implications. A salesperson who aligns belief with behavior achieves higher sales and experiences greater job satisfaction and personal growth. They become a magnet for success, attracting clients and opportunities with ease.

But what is the real-world relevance of these concepts? In an ever-evolving marketplace, aligning belief and behavior has never been more critical. In an age where consumers are more informed and discerning, authenticity sells. The salesperson who genuinely believes in their offering and acts accordingly will stand out in a sea of mediocrity.

What, then, can we learn from the tale of Tom from our previous discussion? His transformation began with a realization and a decision to bring his beliefs and behaviors into harmony. It is a testament to the transformative power that lies within the grasp of every salesperson.

Imagine waking up each day with a clear conviction about your ability to impact your clients' lives positively. Now, envision yourself acting on that conviction—calling leads enthusiastically, crafting proposals carefully, and closing deals with integrity. This is the essence of next-level selling. This is the life that beckons when you resolve the sales dilemma of belief versus behavior.

As we continue our journey through this book, remember that each chapter is not just a collection of words but a mirror reflecting the choices that stand before you. What beliefs will you embrace? What behaviors will you change? The answers lie within you, ready to be unlocked.

As you ponder these questions, let me ask: Are you ready to align your beliefs with your behaviors and step into a new realm of selling and living? Are you prepared to transcend the ordinary and embrace the extraordinary?

The path to 'Next Level Selling - Next Level Life' is paved with your daily decisions. Choose wisely, act boldly, and watch as the world of sales—and life—opens its doors to you.

CHAPTER 7

MASTERING THE ART OF CONSULTATIVE CLOSING

Understanding the Consultative Closing

In the bustling arena of modern sales, the art of closing deals is often viewed as the pinnacle of success. Yet, a revolutionary approach called consultative closing emerges in this evolving customer needs and expectations. This technique signifies the end of a transaction and heralds the beginning of a valuable and long-lasting relationship between the seller and the buyer.

To fully embrace the essence of consultative closing, it is imperative to comprehend the terminology that forms its foundation. Words such as 'value', 'partnership', 'needs analysis', 'solution selling', and 'trust' are not merely jargon; they are the threads that weave the fabric of this sophisticated sales strategy.

Value, a term that echoes through the corridors of sales conversations, transcends the simple notion of worth. In the realm of consultative closing, it embodies the bespoke benefits and tailored solutions that align perfectly with the client's unique requirements and aspirations. The emphasis here is on crafting an offering that resonates with the client's idea of success, not just on price or features.

Partnership paints a picture of a collaborative alliance, where the salesperson and the client embark on a journey together, united by a mutual goal. This relationship is nurtured beyond the transaction, focusing on a strategic alignment where both parties benefit from each other's success.

Needs analysis is the meticulous process of dissecting the client's situation to unearth their true challenges and objectives. Like a skilled surgeon with a scalpel, the salesperson delves into the client's business landscape, identifying pain points and opportunities that might have otherwise remained hidden.

Solution selling, a term that dovetails with consultative closing, shifts the focus from products to problems. Here, the salesperson assumes the role of a problem-solver, crafting customized solutions that address the specific needs unveiled during the needs analysis phase.

Trust, the cornerstone of any meaningful relationship, becomes the currency of consultative closing. It is earned over time through consistency, integrity, and genuine concern for the client's welfare. Trust transforms a salesperson from a mere vendor into a trusted advisor.

Now, imagine a world where these concepts are not abstract but as tangible as the keyboard under your fingertips or the comforting aroma of your morning coffee. In this world, value is the satisfaction that surges within you as you find the perfect fit for your needs. Partnership is the camaraderie you share with colleagues as you work towards a common goal. Needs analysis is the introspection you undertake when facing a complex decision. Solution selling is the advice you seek from a friend who listens and responds to your unique situation. And trust is the unspoken bond you have with someone who has never let you down.

In the grand tapestry of sales, consultative closing is not a mere tactic; it is a philosophy, a mindset that prioritizes the client's success as the ultimate victory. It is the understanding that sales are not about pushing a product but about gathering resources, insights, and expertise to empower the client.

With each interaction, the salesperson employing consultative closing becomes less of a talking brochure and more of a listening partner. They navigate through the murky waters of client hesitations with the grace of a seasoned sailor, acknowledging concerns and offering solutions with the precision of an archer.

The dance of consultative closing is intricate, requiring the salesperson to be attuned to the subtle cues of the client's body language, the cadence of their voice, and the unspoken words behind their questions. "What truly matters to you?" the salesperson might ask, inviting the client into a shared understanding and clarity space.

In a solitary, reflective moment, consider the last time you felt truly heard, truly understood. That feeling valued and supported is the essence of consultative closing. It is not about the rush of victory but the steady build of a relationship that stands the test of time and change.

As the chapter on understanding the consultative closing unfolds, remember that this is more than a sales strategy; it is an approach to life that champions empathy, connection, and genuine concern for the well-being of others. It is an invitation to step into the next level of selling and, by extension, the next level of living.

Pre-Closing Strategies

The journey toward closing is punctuated by critical moments that can make or break a deal. Pre-closing strategies are the foundation for successful closings, shaping the client's experience and solidifying the relationship between buyer and seller. This chapter is your blueprint to laying a robust groundwork that ensures your sales process culminates in a harmonious close, paving the way for a fruitful, ongoing partnership.

Establish the Goal:

Your mission is to master the art of pre-closing, which involves a sequence of targeted actions that will lead you seamlessly to the final agreement. The goal is to create an environment of trust and certainty where the client is primed and ready to affirm the partnership with a resounding "yes."

Necessary Materials or Prerequisites:

Before embarking on this journey, you'll need a thorough understanding of your client's industry, business model, and specific challenges. Arm yourself with a comprehensive profile of the decision-makers, a clear grasp of your product's advantages, and a flexible strategy that can adapt to evolving client needs.

Begin with a Broad Overview:

Pre-closing is a dance of delicate moves, starting with rapport building, advancing through value demonstration, and culminating in subtle confirmations that lead to the ultimate close. It's about nurturing the seeds of agreement well before you present the final proposal.

Detailed Steps:

1. Build a Connection: Begin by fostering a genuine bond with your client. Show interest in their business and personal growth, actively listen to their concerns, and respond with empathy. This is the soil in which trust will flourish.

2. Highlight the Value: Articulate your solution's unique benefits tailored to the client's specific needs. Make it clear how your product or service will solve their problems and help them achieve their goals.

3. Align Visions: Ensure that your client's vision and your proposition are in lockstep. Discuss the future, emphasizing how your solution will continue to serve them down the line.

4. Gain Incremental Agreement: Throughout your interactions, seek small confirmations that the client is on board with your presenting ideas and solutions. These nods of agreement are the stepping stones to the final close.

5. Set the Stage for Decision-Making: Guide the client toward envisioning the decision-making process. Discuss timelines and what the next steps will look like once they decide to move forward.

Tips and Warnings:

- Nurture patience. Pre-closing is a marathon, not a sprint.
- Listen more than you speak. The client's words can guide your strategy.
- Avoid over-promising. Set realistic expectations to maintain credibility.
- Be attuned to non-verbal cues. They often speak louder than words.

Testing or Validation:

A successful pre-close is validated by the client's readiness to proceed. You'll know you're on the right track when the client discusses the implementation and the next steps without prompting.

Troubleshooting (optional):

If the client seems hesitant, revisit earlier conversations to address unresolved issues. Ask open-ended questions to uncover lingering doubts and respond with tailored reassurances and evidence of your solution's result.

As you weave through the tapestry of pre-closing strategies, your sentences should dance to the rhythm of your client's needs, each paragraph a step closer to mutual agreement. Imagine vividly painting a picture where the client sees your solution in their future as clearly as the morning sun. Ask them directly: "How do you see this fitting into your growth plan?" Let their answers guide your strategy, using simple language to keep the path clear and free of obstacles.

Let a one-line paragraph strike the gong of importance when emphasizing a point, like the resounding affirmation of a well-earned trust. And remember, the power of a well-placed quote or anecdote can spark inspiration or relatability that bridges any gap in understanding.

In the journey of pre-closing, you are not just selling a product; you are offering a vision of success, a tapestry where your solution is an integral thread. Show, don't tell. Let your client discover the beauty of your offering through the stories of those who have walked this path before them, the promise of a partnership that elevates their business, and the assurance that with your help, their next level is within reach.

Identifying Buying Signals

The ability to discern a prospect's readiness to commit is akin to having a sixth sense. It's not about what they say outright; it's about interpreting the subtleties, the nuanced signals that whisper, "I'm ready." This chapter is your masterclass in identifying these pivotal buying signals, ensuring you can artfully navigate the conversation toward a successful close.

As we embark on this journey, remember that the essence of sales is not in the hard sell but in the art of listening and observation. The signals are there, like stars waiting to be read by a seasoned astronomer. So, shall we begin our exploration of the celestial cues of closing?

Buying signals are the constellations in the sales universe that, once recognized, guide you to the moment of decision. They are:

1. Verbal affirmations
2. Increased questioning
3. Requests for specifics
4. Sharing of timeframes
5. Discussing decision processes
6. Physical engagement
7. Changes in tone or pace

Let us dive deeper into these celestial signs, decoding their meanings better to align our sales strategies with the prospect's orbit.

Verbal Affirmations

Verbal affirmations are the nods of ascent in the dialogue, the 'yes', 'I see', or 'that makes sense' responses that frequently punctuate your conversation. They are micro-commitments, subtle endorsements of the path you're collectively treading.

Evidence of this can often be found in recorded sales calls where a symphony of such affirmations precedes successful closes. Testimonials from seasoned sales professionals frequently highlight how these verbal cues signaled their cue to pivot toward closing the conversation.

Practical applications of identifying verbal affirmations involve actively listening and mirroring the prospect's language. This shows that you are in tune with them reinforces their positive sentiment towards the offering.

Increased Questioning

An uptick in a prospect's questions signals heightened interest. It's as if the flame of curiosity has been fanned, and now they seek the warmth of understanding. They inquire about features and benefits and often delve into the practicalities of implementation.

Statistics show that prospects who ask detailed questions are more likely to be considering a purchase. Use this opportunity to reinforce the value proposition and address any concerns they might have.

In practice, welcome these questions with open arms. Respond clearly and confidently, ensuring each answer fortifies the prospect's inclination to buy.

Requests for Specifics

When a prospect asks for specific details about pricing, implementation, or customization, they are signaling a move from abstract interest to concrete consideration. They envision your product or service in their ecosystem and examine the fit.

Case studies reveal that deals are 65% more likely to close when a prospect has requested detailed information. This is a golden opportunity to provide tailored responses that align with their unique needs.

Practically, prepare collateral that you can share promptly when such requests arise. This demonstrates preparedness and a willingness to meet the prospect's needs.

Sharing of Timeframes

A prospect who discloses their purchasing timeline is sharing a piece of their strategic planning with you. They are essentially giving you a window into their decision-making world.

Data suggests that timeframes are discussed in the latter stages of the buying process. This is a strong indication that the prospect is seriously considering an investment.

Practically speaking, align your follow-up and closing strategies with the prospect's timeline. This shows respect for their process and positions you as a facilitator rather than an impediment.

Discussing Decision Processes

When discussions turn to the inner workings of the prospect's decision-making process, you are invited into the sanctum of their business considerations. They may begin to outline approval structures or procurement protocols.

Insights from successful sales professional's pinpoint this as a moment to shift gears toward closing strategies. The prospect is ready to discuss 'how,' not just 'if.'

In application, provide clear, concise information to aid them in their process. Be a resource, not a hurdle.

Physical Engagement

Physical cues are the body's way of speaking. A forward lean, a nod, the mirroring of your gestures—these are all signs of engagement and rapport.

Studies in body language suggest that such physical engagement is a precursor to agreement. It signifies a subconscious alignment with the person and the proposition they represent.

In practice, be observant and responsive to these cues. If a prospect leans in, they invite closeness and, by extension, an agreement.

Changes in Tone or Pace

Finally, be attuned to the music of the conversation—the shifts in tone, pace, and volume. Excitement, hesitation, or urgency can all be detected in the voice and can guide your approach.

Research in communication patterns indicates that a prospect's shift towards a more animated or urgent tone is often an indicator of readiness to move forward.

Practically, adjust your communication to complement theirs. Matching their urgency or excitement can create a harmonious exchange, propelling the conversation toward a close.

Aren't these signals like stars guiding a sailor to the shore? With each signal you recognize, you're one step closer to the harbor of success. But remember, the art of interpretation is as much about intuition as it is about evidence. Listen intently, observe closely, and engage thoughtfully.

In the canvas of sales, these buying signals are your palette, and your skill in interpreting them is your brushstroke. Paint your prospect a picture showing the product and allow them to envision the masterpiece of success it will help them create. Show them through stories of triumph, the vivid imagery of a future made brighter with your solution, and the engaging dance of a conversation that inevitably leads to a shared crescendo of agreement.

Let each sentence be a step in this dance, each paragraph a turn towards understanding, and each chapter a milestone in the journey.

Effective Questioning Techniques

Effective questioning is the scalpel of sales – precise, deliberate, and, when wielded with skill, capable of unveiling the core of your prospect's true needs and desires. As you master the art of inquiry, you will guide your prospects toward the close and elevate your interactions, transforming sales into a collaborative journey toward solutions that resonate deeply with their aspirations.

Your ultimate objective is to harness the power of strategic questioning to foster engagement, uncover underlying needs, and lead your prospects to realize that your offering is the key to their challenges. By the end of this process, you will be adept at crafting questions that illuminate the path to a mutually beneficial partnership.

Before you embark on this journey of inquiry, ensure that you are equipped with the following:

- An in-depth understanding of your product or service.
- Insight into your prospect's industry, company, and role.
- Active listening skills to discern the nuances of your prospect's responses.
- A mindset of curiosity and empathy.
- The agility to pivot your questioning based on the conversation's flow.

The roadmap to effective questioning can be conceptualized in four phases:

1. Opening with rapport-building questions.
2. Uncovering needs with probing questions.
3. Deepening understanding with clarifying questions.

4. Steering towards commitment with implication questions.

Opening with Rapport-Building Questions

Your initial questions should be like the gentle strokes of an artist's brush – designed to set the tone and establish a connection. "How has your day been?" or "What inspired you to get into your line of work?" are questions that demonstrate genuine interest and begin the process of building trust.

As you gather these initial insights, observe the subtle shifts in your prospect's demeanor. A relaxed posture or a brightening smile can signal a readiness to open up further, encouraging you to delve deeper.

Uncovering Needs with Probing Questions

Once a rapport is established, it's time to direct the conversation towards your prospect's needs. Probing questions are the catalyst for discovery; they ignite a reaction that can reveal your prospect's challenges. "What challenges are you currently facing in your role?" or "How do these challenges affect your team's productivity?" are questions that encourage your prospect to reflect and share meaningful information.

Remember, when pulled with care, each response is a thread that can unravel the tapestry of your prospect's situation, exposing the patterns and colors of their needs.

Deepening Understanding with Clarifying Questions

With the foundation laid, clarifying questions help you paint a more vivid picture of your prospect's circumstances. "Can you elaborate on how this issue impacts your daily operations?" or "What have you tried in the past to address this problem?" These inquiries are not merely for your illumination but also guide your prospect to a deeper self-examination.

Each answer adds depth to your understanding, sharpening the image of how your product or service can be the brushstroke that transforms their challenge into a masterpiece of efficient solutions.

Steering Towards Commitment with Implication Questions

As the dialogue progresses, implication questions subtly shift the focus towards the positive impact of your solution. "How would overcoming this challenge change your team's output?" or "What would it mean for your company to resolve this issue once and for all?" These questions plant seeds of realization, allowing your prospect to envision the transformative potential of your offering.

With each implication question, you're not merely selling a product but framing a future where your solution is an integral part of their success story.

A word of caution: while powerful questions must be wielded with finesse. Bombarding your prospect with inquiries can overwhelm and create resistance. Balance is key – ask a question, listen intently, and allow the conversation to breathe. Your patience will pay dividends as your prospect feels heard and valued.

Our validation comes from witnessing your prospect's 'aha' moments – those instances where clarity dawns, and they begin to articulate the value of your solution unprompted. In these moments, you realize your questions have successfully led them to the decision threshold.

Not every prospect will be responsive to your line of questioning. If you encounter reluctance, it may be time to reassess your approach. Reflect on whether your questions are too direct, too numerous, or perhaps not sufficiently tailored to the individual. Adjust your strategy, accordingly, always aiming to align with your prospect's communication style and comfort level.

As you close this chapter, reflect on the artistry of your questioning; just as a sculptor chisels away at the marble to reveal the form within, your strategic questions chip away at surface-level interactions, revealing your prospects' deeper needs and aspirations. When you master this art, you don't just sell products; you co-create visions of success.

Handling Objections Gracefully

Objections are not merely knots to be untangled but opportunities for a deeper connection. They emerge on the horizon like challenging peaks, daunting yet conquerable with the right approach. As you stand at the foothills of client hesitation, remember that overcoming objections is not about pressure but understanding, empathy, and finesse.

Imagine yourself as a navigator, charting a course through the waters of doubt and resistance. Your prospect's objections are not barriers but beacons, signaling areas that require your attention and care. Let's explore how to navigate these waters with grace and effectiveness.

In the sales world, objections are as common as the changing tides. Whether it's concern over cost, the perceived complexity of the product, or simply resistance to change, every salesperson will face these hurdles. It's a pivotal moment where the relationship with the prospect hangs in the balance.

But what exactly is the problem? The crux of the issue lies not in the objections but in the salesperson's response. A misstep in objection handling can erode trust and derail the entire selling process. Conversely, a well-navigated objection can strengthen the bond and bring the prospect closer to a yes.

Left unchecked, objections can fester, turning simple concerns into insurmountable barriers. A prospective person who feels unheard or pressured may retreat, taking their business elsewhere. The consequence of mishandled objections isn't just a lost sale— it's a tarnished relationship that could have rippled into future opportunities.

The solution, therefore, is a method of handling objections that is respectful, consultative, and, ultimately, collaborative. It's about shifting the mindset from selling to helping, telling to listening, overcoming to understanding.

How does one implement this graceful approach to objections? Begin with active listening. When a prospect voices an objection, resist the urge to jump in with a counterpoint. Instead, listen intently. Let them know their concerns are valid and understood. "I hear what you're saying, and I understand why that's a concern for you" is a powerful way to acknowledge their feelings.

Next, probe gently to uncover the root of the objection. Sometimes, what's presented on the surface masks a deeper issue. Ask clarifying questions to understand the true nature of their hesitation. "Can you tell me more about why that concerns you?" This opens the door for a deeper conversation and demonstrates your genuine interest in their perspective.

Once the core of the objection is clear, align with the prospect by empathizing with their situation. "I can see how that would be worrying," shows that you're on their side. Then, pivot to introduce how your product or service can alleviate that specific concern. Share stories of how others have faced similar objections and succeeded with your solution. These narratives create a vivid image of potential and possibility.

Evidence of your solution's effectiveness comes from real-life examples. Share case studies, testimonials, or data that illustrate the positive outcomes others have experienced. "When Company X implemented our solution, they saw a 30% reduction in the issue you're concerned about." can be an eye-opening revelation for a tentative prospect.

It's essential to acknowledge that there are always alternatives.

Perhaps, in some cases, your solution isn't the perfect fit, and that's okay. By discussing other options, you not only showcase your industry knowledge but also build credibility. "While our product does X and Y, if you're looking for Z, then this other solution might be better suited for you" is a statement that exudes confidence and integrity.

Remember to maintain a cadence that resonates with your prospect as you weave through the intricate dance of addressing objections. Let your words flow with sincerity, and your pauses offer them space to reflect and respond. In this rhythm, a mutual understanding is formed, and the path to agreement is paved.

Whether you're exchanging emails, conversing over the phone, or sitting across the table from your prospect, each interaction is a brushstroke in the larger picture of your relationship. By handling objections gracefully, you're not merely inching closer to a sale— you're crafting a narrative of partnership, trust, and success.

Ultimately, it's not about the art of the deal but the art of the journey. When you master the ability to navigate objections with grace, you're not just selling a product; you're offering a gateway to a next-level life for your prospects and, indeed, for yourself.

Closing With Confidence: Tips and Tricks

The final act of sealing the deal can often be the most daunting. But what if you could approach the close with the same confidence as a seasoned performer taking the stage? This is not just a distant dream but an attainable reality. The ability to close with confidence is not an innate talent bestowed upon a select few; it's a skill that can be honed and mastered with the right set of techniques. In the following pages, you will discover a collection of actionable tips that will empower you to end your sales conversations on a triumphant note.

A Preview of the Pivotal Points

1. Establish a Connection
2. Recognize Buying Signals
3. Use Assumptive Closes
4. Address Last-Minute Hesitations
5. Implement the 'Now or Never' Close

Establish a Connection The Foundation of Trust:

Building rapport with your client forms the bedrock of a successful close. Establishing a connection goes beyond mere pleasantries; it's about creating a relationship predicated on trust and mutual respect. To foster this bond, engage with your client's needs, listen actively to their concerns, and personalize your interactions. When clients feel understood, they are more likely to trust your recommendations and be receptive to the closing process.

Trust is not given; it's earned. And in the competitive world of sales, earning trust is paramount. Show genuine interest in your client's business and personal goals. Take notes during conversations and reference them in future interactions. This attention to detail demonstrates that you value the relationship, not just the transaction.

Consider the story of a sales representative who, by remembering a client's upcoming vacation and inquiring about it, built a rapport that eventually led to a multi-deal contract. The client said, "I chose to work with you because you didn't just see me as another sale. You saw me as a person."

In your next sales meeting, take a moment to ask a personal question or reference a previous conversation instead of diving straight into your pitch. This simple act can create a more meaningful and productive dialogue.

Once a solid foundation of trust is established, recognizing when a client is ready to buy becomes the next critical step in the closing process.

Recognize Buying Signals
Decoding the Unspoken:

Clients often communicate their readiness to buy through subtle cues and behavioral shifts. It's essential to attune your senses to these buying signals, such as increased engagement, asking detailed questions about implementation, or discussing potential timelines. Identifying these signals allows you to tailor your closing approach to the client's readiness.

Buying signals can be verbal or nonverbal. A verbal signal might be a question about how the product can be tailored to their needs, indicating they envision using your solution. Nonverbal cues could include nods of agreement or leaning in, reflecting interest and agreement.

A sales veteran recounts how a client, initially reserved, began asking about specific features and how they could be applied within their organization. Recognizing this turn in the conversation as a buying signal, the salesperson shifted gears to discuss closing terms, leading to a successful sale.

During your following sales conversation, pay close attention to what is said and what remains unspoken. Look for engagement and readiness and be prepared to move toward the close when these signals emerge.

Recognizing that a client is ready to buy is half the battle. The next step is guiding them towards committing using assumptive closes.

Use Assumptive Closes
The Gentle Guide:

The assumptive close is a technique where you proceed as if the client has already decided to buy, subtly nudging them towards the sale. This is not about being presumptuous or pushy but about framing the conversation in a way that assumes a positive outcome.

An effective assumptive close might involve discussing the next steps after purchase or discussing implementation strategies. This approach can minimize resistance as it shifts the client's mindset from deciding whether to buy to considering the logistics of the purchase.

Research shows that when salespeople use assumptive language, such as "When would be the best time to schedule the installation?" rather than "Would you like to proceed with the purchase?" the likelihood of a positive response increases significantly.

In your upcoming sales interactions, practice framing your language to reflect the assumption of a sale. Observe how this subtle shift in approach can change the dynamic of the conversation.

Even with a strong assumptive close, clients may have lastminute hesitations. It's crucial to address these effectively to maintain momentum.

Address Last-Minute Hesitations
Overcoming the Eleventh-Hour Obstacle:

No matter how smooth the sales process is, last-minute hesitations can arise. These can stem from various concerns, from budget constraints to fear of change. It's important not to dismiss these hesitations but to address them head-on with empathy and assurance.

Listen to your client's concerns without interruption. Reiterate their points to show understanding and provide clear, concise information to alleviate their worries. If the concern is budget, discuss the return on investment. If it's about change, highlight support systems in place to facilitate a smooth transition.

A sales professional shares a success story where a client's worry about implementation complexity was quelled by a custom tailored onboarding process, ultimately leading to a confident closing.

Next time a client hesitates, validate their concern, offer a solution, and ask if this addresses their worry. This approach can help clear the path to a confident close.

While addressing hesitations is critical, sometimes a sense of urgency is required to motivate the client to act. This is where the 'Now or Never' close can be particularly impactful.

Implement the 'Now or Never' Close
Creating a Sense of Urgency·

The 'Now or Never' close is a tactic used to prompt immediate action by introducing a time-sensitive element. This could be a limited-time offer, a discount, or a special bonus that expires soon. The key is to create a compelling reason for the client to act now rather than later.

This technique must be used sparingly and ethically, ensuring that the urgency you're creating is genuine. Clients can sense insincerity, and you never want to sacrifice trust for the sake of a quick sale.

A study in consumer behavior found that time-limited offers can significantly increase the likelihood of purchase as they tap into the natural human tendency to avoid missing out.

If you decide to use a 'Now or Never' close, make sure the offer is attractive and relevant to the client. Be transparent about the timeframe and the benefits of acting promptly.

In closing, it's important to remember that confidence in sales comes from preparation, understanding your client, and mastering the techniques that lead to successful outcomes. By integrating these tips into your sales strategy, you can approach each closing opportunity with the assurance of a seasoned professional and the heart of a trusted advisor. The close is not just the end of a sales conversation; it's the beginning of a new level of partnership and success. Are you ready to take the next step and elevate your closing game to the next level?

Consultative Closing Case Studies

The art of consultative closing stands out as a masterstroke that transforms transactions into enduring partnerships. It's a strategic dance that balances the seller's expertise with the buyer's unique needs, culminating in a mutually beneficial agreement. Within these pages lies a tapestry of real-world victories, a testament to the power of consultative closing.

Imagine a bustling tech startup in Silicon Valley, its open-plan office buzzing with the electric hum of innovation. The walls are plastered with whiteboards scrawled with code and strategy, and the air crackles with the energy of dreams being built byte by byte. Here, we meet Sophia, a sales director with a keen mind for problem-solving, and her client, a behemoth in the telecommunications industry looking to overhaul its customer service platform.

The challenge at hand was formidable. The client had been grappling with an outdated system, leading to customer frustrations and dwindling satisfaction scores. Sophia's task was to convince them that her company's cutting-edge software was an upgrade and a revolution for their customer service operations.

The approach Sophia took was methodical and consultative.

She began by immersing herself in the client's world, spending days observing their customer service reps and understanding the pain points from the ground up. She crafted a solution that addressed their current issues and scaled for future growth while aligning with their long-term strategic goals.

When the time came to present her proposal, Sophia painted a vivid picture of a future where call wait times were slashed and customer satisfaction soared. She backed her vision with robust data, illustrating a projected increase in customer retention rates and a significant reduction in operational costs.

The results were nothing short of spectacular. Within six months of implementing Sophia's solution, the client saw a 25% increase in customer satisfaction and a 40% reduction in call wait times. Their customer service reps reported higher job satisfaction, and the ripple effects were felt company wide.

Reflecting on this triumph, one can glean insights into the essence of consultative closing. It's not just about meeting sales targets; It's about deeply understanding the client's needs and crafting a solution that resonates on a fundamental level. It is about partnership and trust.

Visual aids included graphs depicting the growth in customer satisfaction and efficiency post-implementation, clearly confirming the strategy's impact.

This case study showcases the success of a single project and echoes the broader narrative of consultative selling as a pillar of modern sales strategy. It underscores the transition from transactional to relational, from selling a product to solving a problem.

So, as we close this chapter, one question lingers in the air: How might the principles of consultative closing revolutionize your approach to selling and elevate your life to the next level? Sophia and her client's story is one example of this transformative power at work. As we turn the page, let us delve deeper into the rich landscape of consultative selling, where every challenge is an opportunity, and every close is a gateway to enduring success.

CHAPTER 8

THE SALES PROCESS DECONSTRUCTED

The Anatomy of a Sales Process

In the hustling bazaar of commerce, the art of selling is often likened to a well-choreographed dance. It is an intricate performance where every step, every gesture, and every pause hold significance. As we dive into the anatomy of a sales process, we uncover the skeletal framework that upholds every successful transaction. This chapter aims to dissect this framework, exploring the tendons and muscles that give it life and motion.

Before peeling back the layers, let us map out the territory we'll traverse. A well-structured sales process typically unfurls across several critical stages. Each stage builds upon the last, creating a cohesive journey that guides both seller and buyer toward a mutually beneficial outcome.

The List and Elaboration structure will serve as our guide. We start with a concise inventory of key points, followed by an in-depth dissection of each. This approach enriches the reader's understanding with layered context and detail. The pivotal points of our journey are as follows:

1. Prospecting and Lead Generation
2. Initial Contact and Rapport Building
3. Needs Assessment and Qualification
4. Presentation and Demonstration
5. Handling Objections
6. Closing the Deal
7. Follow-up and Relationship Management

With the trail set before us, let's venture into the heart of the matter.

The journey begins with prospecting, the quest to identify potential customers — your leads. This stage is the bedrock upon which all else is built, for without leads, there can be no sales, and without sales, there can be no success.

Prospecting is a meticulous process that involves market research, networking, and strategic outreach. Sales professionals must cast a wide net yet remain discerning, targeting individuals or organizations with a certain potential for need or interest in the product or service offered.

Data-driven approaches and firsthand accounts underscore the importance of this stage. According to a study by the RAIN Group, high-performing sales organizations are twice as likely to prioritize lead generation efforts compared to their average-performing counterparts.

When put into practice, effective prospecting might involve leveraging social media platforms, attending industry events, or utilizing referral programs. These practical applications ensure a steady pipeline of opportunities, fueling the subsequent stages of the sales process.

After identifying potential leads, forging a connection becomes the crux of the next stage. Initial contact with a potential customer marks the first impression, which can set the tone for the entire sales relationship.

The key to this stage is authenticity. Building rapport is not just about making small talk; it's about genuinely understanding the client's world — their challenges, successes, and aspirations. Sellers who excel at this stage often approach each interaction with empathy and curiosity.

What does this look like in the field? Imagine a sales rep who remembers a client's recent vacation and asks about it or one who shares a relevant article on a topic they know the client is passionate about. These small gestures speak volumes, paving the way for trust and open dialogue.

Thoroughly understanding a client's needs is vital, yet determining whether they are the right fit for your offering is equally important. This dual assessment and qualification process ensures that time and effort are invested wisely.

During this stage, sharp questioning skills come to the fore. Salespeople should ask probing questions that reveal what the client wants and why they want it. This depth of understanding allows for tailored solutions that resonate on a personal level.

Evidence of the significance of this stage comes from countless successful sales strategies that prioritize consultative selling, emphasizing the salesperson's role as a trusted advisor.

In real-world scenarios, a sales rep might use CRM systems to record and analyze customer data, ensuring that the proposed solutions align perfectly with the client's needs and potential for long-term value.

With a clear understanding of the client's needs, the salesperson can now present the product or service in a way that speaks directly to those needs. In this stage, features are translated into benefits, and value propositions become vividly clear.

A masterful presentation is not a monologue; it's an interactive experience that invites the customer to envision the positive impact the product or service will have on their life or business.

Testimonials and case studies often play a crucial role here, providing credible evidence of the product's benefits and bolstering the salesperson's claims.

The practical application of this stage might involve customizing a demo to show exactly how a software solution would streamline the client's workflow or offering a sample that allows the client to experience the product first-hand.

Even the smoothest presentations can encounter resistance. Handling objections is an art form that requires a good ear and a nimble mind. The goal is not to overpower objections but to understand and address them.

This stage is marked by active listening and empathetic responses. Skilled salespeople treat objections not as roadblocks but as opportunities to clarify further and underscore the value proposition.

The real-life application involves anticipating common objections and preparing thoughtful, evidence-backed responses. It also means staying adaptable and ready to engage in a constructive dialogue that moves the conversation forward.

The penultimate stage is the crescendo of the sales process — closing the deal. This is where all prior efforts culminate, and the salesperson must be decisive yet tactful, ensuring the client feels confident and satisfied with their decision.

Closing techniques vary, but they all hinge on timing and perception. Recognizing the moment when a client is ready to commit is as important as the words used to seal the commitment.

Practical applications include trial closes to gauge readiness, summarizing key benefits to reinforce the decision, and offering incentives that make saying "yes" even more attractive.

The sales process does not end with a closed deal; it simply evolves. Follow-up and ongoing relationship management are the lifeblood of future sales and referrals.

Consistent, value-added communication ensures that customers feel valued and supported long after the ink has dried on the contract. This stage is about nurturing a long-term partnership that can lead to repeat business and organic growth through word-of- mouth.

In practice, this may involve customer satisfaction surveys, personalized check-ins, and loyalty programs designed to keep the relationship vibrant and the client engaged.

As we step back and survey the anatomy of a sales process, it's clear that each stage is integral, each connection critical. By understanding and mastering these stages, sales professionals can elevate their craft, transforming transactions into relationships and prospects into partners.

Consider this: Are you ready to dissect your sales process to fine-tune each stage for optimum performance? The journey to next-level selling — and, indeed, a next-level life — begins with the courage to ask such questions and the commitment to pursue their answers.

Prospecting and Lead Generation

Stepping into the limelight of the sales arena, where prospects are the lifeblood that fuels the growth engine of any business, we come to understand that the art of attracting potential clients is akin to casting a net in the vast ocean of the marketplace. It requires skill, an understanding of the currents, and the right tools. Prospecting and lead generation, therefore, are not merely about reaching out. They are about reaching out effectively, strategically, and with a high touch that resonates with those most likely to become customers and loyal advocates for your brand.

As the reader, you are about to embark on a journey that will amplify your ability to find and allure the clientele that will take your business to unparalleled heights. With each step, you'll be building a bridge between your company's offerings and your target market's needs. The goal is clear: cultivating a thriving garden of leads that will blossom into a bountiful harvest of sales.

Let's establish a foundation before we cut into the fabric of this process. To navigate this endeavor, you will need a deep understanding of your product or service, a clear profile of your ideal customer, a set of tools for capturing and managing leads, and a strategy for reaching out to these potential clients. This arsenal is your key to unlocking a world brimming with opportunities.

Take a moment now to visuallze the journey ahead. Picture a map with a starting point labeled "Prospecting" and a series of pathways leading to various destinations named "Lead Nurturing," "Engagement," and ultimately "Conversion." This map is your broad overview, a snapshot of the terrain you'll traverse, marked with landmarks that signify each pivotal phase of the lead generation journey.

Let's embark on the adventure, starting with the detailed steps to guide you through each process phase.

Imagine stepping into a bustling marketplace. The blaring of sights, sounds, and scents immediately engulfs your senses. Prospecting, the initial phase, is much like entering this space with a keen sense of purpose. You must sift through the multitude, identifying those who exhibit even a hint of interest in what you have to offer. Begin with research; understand the demographics and psychographics of your ideal customer. Then, engage in targeted outreach through social media, content marketing, and networking events. Each interaction is a thread woven into the larger tapestry of your lead generation efforts.

As you garner interest, it's time to capture these leads. Employ tools such as CRM systems, email capture forms, and call-to-action buttons strategically placed on your website and social media platforms. These tools are not just receptacles for information; they are the vessels that carry prospects through the nurturing process.

A word of caution: as you cast your net wide, remember not all fish are worth the catch. Qualify your leads to ensure your efforts are concentrated on those with the highest potential for conversion. Ask yourself: Does this prospect have a need my product can fulfill?

Do they have the authority and means to make a purchase? Is there a sense of urgency? Qualification is the sieve that separates the chaff, leaving you with the golden grains of promising prospects.

But how do you know if your strategies are effective? Testing and validation are crucial. Monitor your conversion rates, track engagement metrics, and solicit feedback. Look for patterns and adjust your approach accordingly. The proof of a successful prospecting and lead-generation strategy lies in the numbers. Is your pool of leads growing? Are those leads moving through the sales funnel?

Should you encounter obstacles, don't lose heart. Troubleshooting is part of the process. Perhaps your message isn't resonating, or your outreach is too broad. Adjust your targeting, refine your message, and test different channels. Remember, every 'no' is a step closer to 'yes.'

As we draw this blueprint for lead generation to a close, consider these final nuggets of wisdom. With every interaction, strive to leave a lasting impression that echoes the value of your offering. Be the beacon that guides your prospects through the fog of countless options to the safe harbor that is your business. This is not just about selling; it's about creating a narrative where your product or service is the hero in each client's success story.

With these strategies and a steadfast commitment to the process, you're not just selling; you're elevating your prospects to the next level of their journey and, in doing so, elevating your own life to a new echelon of excellence.

Qualifying Leads: A Critical Step

A discerning eye is vital. Amongst the eager crowd, only a select few carry the promise of becoming not just customers but pillars of business growth. This is where the art of qualifying leads becomes the sharpened tool in your sales arsenal, an indispensable step that requires both finesse and strategic insight. This chapter unfolds the vital lead qualification process, ensuring your sales efforts are as effective and efficient as possible.

Qualifying leads is akin to sifting gold from silt; it requires patience, skill, and the right techniques. The concept is straightforward: it's about identifying which prospects have the potential to buy and are a good fit for your offering. The idea is not to pursue every lead but to focus your energies on those most likely to convert into customers, optimizing your time and resources.

Let's dig into the practical aspects of this process with a real-world example. Imagine you're at a networking event, exchanging pleasantries and business cards. Among the numerous contacts you make, there's one individual whose business needs align perfectly with the services you provide. This is the moment where lead qualification comes into play. You ask targeted questions to gauge their interest level, assess their decision-making power, and understand their timeline for purchasing. This interaction is a miniature case study of qualifying leads in action.

It's essential to consider different perspectives on qualifying leads. Some sales professionals advocate for a volume approach, pursuing many leads to increase the probability of sales. Others suggest a more targeted method, focusing on high-quality leads with a higher chance of conversion. The balance lies in understanding your market, sales cycle, and capacity to manage leads.

Statistical evidence underscores the importance of qualifying leads. According to research, companies with well-defined lead qualification processes experience a 50% higher conversion rate than those that do not. This compelling data points to the significant impact proper lead qualification can have on your bottom line.

As you navigate through the intricate web of lead qualification, it's crucial to clarify terms that might seem esoteric. For instance, the term 'BANT'—which stands for Budget, Authority, Need, and Timeline—is a widely used framework to evaluate the viability of a lead. Let's break down BANT to its core elements: Does the prospect have the Budget to afford your product or service? Do they have the Authority to make purchasing decisions? Is there a genuine need for your solution? And what is the Timeline for the potential purchase? Understanding BANT is essential for effective lead qualification.

In conclusion, the importance of qualifying leads cannot be overstated. It's a critical step that ensures your sales efforts are not squandered on fruitless endeavors. Remember, a well-qualified lead is like a seed that can grow into a strong, fruitful relationship with your business. By focusing on the right prospects, you increase your chances of success and pave the way for a more sustainable and profitable sales process.

As you turn the page on this chapter, remember that qualifying leads is not just a task—it's a strategic approach to elevating your business. The careful selection of opportunities will enable you to reach the next level in sales and, ultimately, in life. In the next chapter, we will explore the dynamics of engaging with these qualified leads and nurturing them into lasting business relationships.

Presentation Skills for Sales Success

A compelling presentation can distinguish between an attentive audience that hangs on to your every word and an indifferent one that slips through the cracks of missed opportunities. Your ability to deliver a powerful presentation is not just a skill; it is an art that, when mastered, can elevate your sales to new heights and enrich your life with success. This chapter is a deep dive into honing your presentation skills, ensuring that your performance captivates, convinces, and converts when the stage is set.

Your goal is clear: to become a maestro of sales presentations. This means captivating your audience from the first word to the last, leaving a lasting impression that resonates and persuades them to act. To achieve this, you need more than just a good pitch; you require a symphony of skills, tools, and processes that work in harmony to deliver a message that is both memorable and effective.

Before you embark on this journey, let's consider the prerequisites. You'll need a deep understanding of your product or service, a keen awareness of your audience's needs and pain points, and a well-crafted message that aligns with those needs. Furthermore, the tools of your trade are pivotal: a slideshow that compliments rather than dominates, handouts that reinforce your message, and any other visual or physical aids that can enhance your delivery.

Visualize the process as a series of steps leading up to a crescendo. Initially, you provide an overview, setting the stage with a preview of what's to come. This is followed by a deep dive into each aspect of your presentation, culminating in a powerful conclusion that leaves no doubt in your audience's minds about your value.

Now, let's peel back the layers of each step.

First, you must craft a narrative that resonates. Begin with an attention-grabbing hook—a startling statistic, a provocative question, or a relatable anecdote. Then, as you weave your story, ensure each point flows logically into the next, building momentum as you go.

As you dive into the substance of your presentation, remember that clarity is king. Clarify your points with precision, using vivid and concise language. Paint pictures with your words, and let those images linger in the minds of your listeners. When discussing features and benefits, don't just list them; show how they come to life in the context of your audience's world.

Sprinkle your delivery with practical advice. For example, when discussing a complex concept, use metaphors to simplify it. Caution your audience against common misconceptions that could cloud their understanding—and, by extension, their decision-making.

How will you know if your presentation has hit the mark? The validation lies in the response you receive. Engage your audience throughout with direct questions, peering into their thoughts and gauging their reactions. The nods, the notes being taken, the thoughtful expressions—all indicate that your message is landing.

Should you encounter questions that challenge your message, don't falter. This is your opportunity to demonstrate expertise and confidence. Offer clear, concise answers, and if a question falls outside the scope of your presentation, acknowledge it and promise a follow-up. This shows professionalism and respect for your audience's curiosity.

A well-prepared speaker is not only an informed one but also an adaptable one. (And I'm also a professional speaker) If you sense a disconnect, don't be afraid to shift gears. Perhaps a story or a quick demonstration can bring back lost attention. Keep your composure and guide your audience back to the core of your message.

As you bring your presentation to a close, do so with a statement that resonates, a call to action that motivates. Your final words should echo in the minds of your audience, compelling them to take the next step.

Remember, your presentation reflects your passion and belief in what you're selling. Let that conviction shine through when you stand before your audience, poised and ready. Each gesture, each word, and each pause play its part in the grand performance of your sales presentation.

In your quest to achieve Next Level presentation skills, these are not just ornaments but essential tools to carve your path to success. As you turn this page, carry with you the knowledge that with each presentation, you are not merely selling a product or service; you are offering a piece of a dream, a vision of what could be. Harness this power and watch as your sales and life transform before your eyes.

Negotiation Tactics for Sales Professionals

The dance of negotiation is intricate and nuanced, a subtle interplay of give and take that, when performed with finesse, can lead to a crescendo of closed deals and satisfied parties. The lifeblood of sales lies not just in presenting a compelling offer but in navigating the ebb and flow of negotiation to reach an agreement that feels like a triumph for all involved. This chapter offers you the keys to reaching the next level in selling by mastering the art of negotiation, thereby enriching your professional life and your own.

Your goal is a lofty yet attainable one: to transform yourself into a par excellence negotiator who closes deals favorably and with a sense of partnership and mutual gain. This is the art of creating value where none seemed to exist, of finding common ground amidst a maze of differing interests.

Before you embark on this journey, you must gather your toolkit. This includes a thorough knowledge of your product or service, a clear understanding of your client's needs and wants a firm grasp of negotiation strategies, and an unwavering confidence in your ability to find a win-win solution.

Picture the negotiation process as a journey through a labyrinth, where each turn represents a potential path toward your desired outcome. Initially, you'll need an aerial view of the maze—a broad overview of the phases you'll navigate.

Let's now embark on the detailed exploration of each phase.

Begin by setting the stage. Research is your guiding star here. Understand your client's business, the industry they operate in, and the challenges they face. Knowledge is power, and in negotiation, it is also leverage.

Next, establish rapport. The foundation of any successful negotiation is trust. Engage in small talk, find common interests, and demonstrate genuine curiosity about your counterpart's perspective. As you build this connection, the negotiation transforms from a transaction to a dialogue.

As you enter the core of the negotiation, remember to listen more than you speak. Uncover the underlying interests behind the positions presented. Often, what is first put on the table is but the tip of the iceberg of what truly matters to your client.

Aim to present your offer not as a fixed package but as a flexible solution tailored to meet your uncovered needs. Highlight the benefits that align with their interests and be prepared to make concessions that cost you little but mean much to the other party.

Throughout the negotiation, sprinkle in practical advice and cautionary tales. For instance, advise against the common pitfall of anchoring too heavily on price. Remind them that value is not just in the numbers but in the relationship and the long-term benefits.

How will you know you've negotiated well? The deal itself is a sign, but so is the relationship you've built. A successful negotiation is one that both parties would willingly enter into again.

Troubleshooting is part of the journey. You might encounter resistance or a stalemate. When this happens, don't panic. Instead, ask open-ended questions that encourage the exploration of alternatives. "What if we..." can open doors that seemed shut.

As you draw the negotiation to a close, do so with confirmation of the value you've both created. Your parting words should reinforce the partnership and the bright future ahead.

Remember, the essence of negotiation is the search for agreement. As you refine your skills, you're not just selling a product or service but sculpting a masterpiece of collaboration. With each successful negotiation, you advance your career and craft a life marked by meaningful connections and achievements.

Embrace this art and watch as the sales world becomes not a battleground but a fertile field where relationships grow and deals flourish. Welcome to the next level of selling, where every negotiation is a step toward a more fulfilling life.

Following Up: The Key to Sales Persistence

The initial conversation is just the opening act of what could be an enthralling performance. (Always take notes) The true artistry lies in the finesse of follow-up, the gentle yet persistent pursuit that can turn a maybe into a resounding yes. For those determined to master the craft of sales, understanding the significance of follow-up is akin to unlocking a secret chamber where deals are nurtured, and relationships are fortified. This chapter is your map to the treasure trove, guiding you through the labyrinthine follow-up process with precision and care, ensuring that your sales persistence pays dividends in both your professional and personal spheres.

Envision yourself achieving higher sales targets and cultivating a garden of ongoing opportunities that bloom long after the initial meeting. This is the goal: to transform the follow-up process into a harmonious extension of your sales strategy that reinforces your commitment to the client and solidifies your reputation as a dedicated professional.

Before embarking on this journey, you must be equipped with essential materials: a detailed record of your interactions with clients, a schedule for follow-up, personalized messaging templates, and a resilient mindset that views follow-up not as a chore but as an opportunity for growth.

Imagine a tapestry woven with intricate threads, each thread representing a follow-up action delicately interlaced to create a striking picture of diligence and attention to detail. Let's take a broad overview of the steps involved: initiating contact post meeting, sending personalized communications, addressing client concerns proactively, and securing the sale with assertive yet respectful persistence.

Now, dive into the detailed steps. Your first action post meeting is a thank you message, a simple yet powerful gesture that sets the tone for future correspondence. Within 24 hours, reach out with an appreciation for the client's time and reiterate key points discussed, ensuring they know you were fully engaged.

Next, schedule a follow-up call. Timing is delicate; too soon, and you may seem overeager; too long, and the lead cools.

Typically, a week is a respectful interval, giving them space to reflect but keeping the dialogue active. Prepare for this call by reviewing notes from your initial meeting and formulating open-ended questions that invite further discussion.

As you weave your way through follow-up communications, personalize each message. For instance, if your client mentioned an upcoming event or achievement, reference it. This shows attentiveness and fosters a deeper connection.

Offer tips, such as suggesting a small tweak to their current process that could yield significant results. But also heed warnings; avoid overwhelming them with messages or calls, as this can tip the scale from persistent to pestering.

Validation of your efforts comes in various forms— a client's enthusiastic response to a follow-up, a confirmed second meeting, or the ultimate prize, a finalized deal. These are the markers that your follow-up strategy is effective.

In the event of troubleshooting, if a client seems disengaged, revisit your approach. Could your messaging be more tailored? Is the timing of your communications optimal? Sometimes, it's not about pushing harder but rather adjusting your tactics.

A final thought to ponder: How can you ensure that your follow-up resonates with authenticity and not just a robotic routine? The answer lies in the genuine belief in the value you offer. When your follow-up is infused with this conviction, it transcends mere persistence—it becomes a testament to your passion for delivering solutions that truly make a difference in your client's lives.

In essence, the key to sales persistence is not just about how many times you follow up but how you conduct each step with purpose and consideration. Next Level Selling is about harnessing the power of follow-up to unlock closed doors, build bridges where gaps seemed too wide, and cultivate a thriving garden where once there were only seeds of possibility. Embrace this key and watch as your sales and life elevate to previously unimagined heights.

Streamlining the Sales Cycle

In today's bustling marketplace, where time is the currency of utmost value, the ability to expedite the sales cycle is akin to discovering a shortcut to the summit of success. Businesses and sales professionals alike grapple with the challenge of shortening the path from prospect to satisfied customer, all while maintaining the integrity of the sales process. When executed with precision, this pursuit accelerates revenue generation and enhances customer satisfaction and loyalty.

Consider the sales cycle as a river, its strong currents and path winding. Every river flows to the sea, but some take a more direct route, conserving energy and arriving with greater force. Similarly, a protracted sales cycle can be a turbulent journey for both the seller and the buyer, fraught with opportunities for disengagement and loss of interest. The key, then, is to channel the flow of this river, reducing meanders and removing obstacles to create a swift and smooth passage to the desired outcome.

What, then, are the potential consequences of a sluggish sales cycle? Picture a fruit left too long upon the branch; it overripens and eventually spoils. In business terms, a deal that lingers excessively on the vine may fall victim to changing market conditions, evolving customer priorities, or competitive encroachment. The cost of delay is multifaceted: lost deals, squandered resources, and a tarnished reputation for efficiency.

To mitigate these risks, one must introduce strategic solutions that trim the excess without compromising quality. The approach must be holistic, looking at the sales cycle from every angle to identify areas ripe for optimization.

Let us embark on this transformative journey by delineating a roadmap for implementation. The first waypoint is the alignment of sales and marketing efforts. By ensuring that marketing materials and sales pitches are in harmony, we create a seamless experience for the prospect, where each interaction builds upon the last, propelling them forward in their decision-making process.

Next, consider the power of qualification. A keen eye can discern between a merely interested lead and one who is ready to engage. Sales teams can avoid the quagmire of unlikely opportunities by focusing energy on high-probability prospects. Employing a set of well-defined qualifying criteria is not only efficient—it is essential.

Furthermore, embrace the digital revolution. The modern buyer is well-informed and often prefers a digital-first interaction. Tools such as CRM software enable sales professionals to track and analyze customer interactions, automating mundane tasks and providing insightful data that can be leveraged to personalize the sales experience.

But what is the evidence to support these propositions? Cast your gaze upon companies that have embraced such strategies, witnessing reductions in their sales cycles by up to 20%. These are not mere anecdotes but quantifiable outcomes, benchmarks for what is possible when strategy aligns with execution.

There are, of course, alternative methods to consider. Some advocate for a more aggressive approach, pushing for rapid closure to capitalize on a prospect's initial interest. Others suggest a meticulous nurturing process, cultivating relationships over time to ensure a deep-rooted commitment. Each strategy has merits and may serve different industries and sales environments effectively.

Enter the one-line paragraph, the distillation of our discourse: The essence of streamlining the sales cycle is the art of balance.

Let us not fall prey to the seduction of complexity. In our pursuit of brevity, let us wield the tools of simplicity and clarity, speaking in a language that resonates with all. Our words must flow with a rhythm that captivates, sentences ebbing and flowing like a melody that stirs the soul.

As we draw this discussion to a close, ponder this: Are your current sales practices a sturdy vessel, navigating the river's course easily, or do they need refinement to harness the currents in your favor? The strategies outlined herein are your oars; with them, you can steer toward the horizon of efficiency, where the next level of selling—and indeed, the next level of life—awaits.

CHAPTER 9

THRIVING ON COMMISSION: OVERCOMING FEAR

The Psychology of Commission-Based Sales

I n the bustling world of sales, one term that often sparks both excitement and apprehension is "commission-based sales." It's a concept that has defined the livelihoods of countless individuals who thrive under the pressure of performance-driven environments.

At its core, commission-based sales is a compensation model where the salesperson's earnings are entirely or predominantly derived from their sales. This means that their income is directly tied to their ability to sell the product or service they represent. Unlike a fixed salary, where earnings are consistent regardless of output, commission-based income fluctuates with sales performance.

The key elements of commission-based sales hinge on motivation, risk, and reward. Sales professionals are motivated by the potential for high earnings but also face the risk of earning little to nothing during lean periods. The reward system is simple yet powerful: the more you sell, the more you earn.

Historically, this model has ancient roots, with evidence suggesting that commission-like structures were in use even in early trading civilizations where merchants would pay agents a share for selling goods in distant markets. The term 'commission' itself comes from the Latin 'committere', meaning 'to entrust'. In essence, sales agents are entrusted with a product or service to sell, and in return, they receive a portion of the proceeds as their reward.

When we contextualize commission-based sales within a broader framework, it becomes clear that it's not just about individual earnings; it shapes business operations and sales strategies. Companies often favor this model as it incentivizes high performance and aligns the salesperson's interests with the companies.

In the real world, commission-based sales are ubiquitous across various industries, from real estate and automotive to software and financial services. A real estate agent, for instance, might earn a percentage of the sale price of a property they help to sell. A car salesman might earn a commission for each vehicle that rolls off the lot, thanks to their efforts.

Despite its prevalence, commission-based sales are often clouded by common misconceptions. Some perceive it as an unstable or unfair payment structure, not recognizing the potential for high rewards that can far exceed traditional salary models. Others might underestimate the level of skill and dedication required to succeed in such a competitive field.

Dive deeper, and you'll discover that commission-based sales are more than just a payment structure—it's a psychological journey. Sales professionals not only master the art of persuasion but also develop resilience to navigate the highs and lows of their earnings.

Why does this model persist, and what drives individuals to choose this path? The allure of uncapped earnings is enticing, but it takes a particular mindset to succeed. The psychology behind commission-based sales is deeply rooted in the human drive for achievement and recognition. This drive is often fueled by goals, whether they're financial, personal growth, or the thrill of closing a deal.

Imagine the adrenaline rush when a sale is confirmed, the satisfaction of seeing your efforts translate into tangible rewards. A profound sense of accomplishment comes from knowing your skills and hard work directly impacts your income.

The landscape of commission-based sales is not without its challenges. The uncertainty of income can be daunting, requiring salespeople to cultivate a level of financial discipline and emotional stability that might not be necessary for more predictable jobs.

Consider the real-life scenario of a sales professional during an economic downturn. The market is sluggish, buyers are hesitant, and the once-steady stream of commission checks slows to a trickle. It's a testing time that probes the salesperson's resolve, creativity, and adaptability. How will they pivot their strategies? Can they maintain a positive outlook?

This brings us to an essential aspect of commission-based sales: resilience. The ability to bounce back from setbacks and persist through dry spells is a hallmark of successful sales professionals. They understand that every 'no' brings them closer to a 'yes' and that each rejection is an opportunity to refine their approach.

In the world of commission-based sales, one-line paragraphs like this hold weight: Resilience is key.

To navigate these psychological waters, one must equip oneself with more than just sales techniques; they must also foster mental toughness and a capacity for continuous learning. It's a dynamic interplay between skill and psychology, where each sale becomes a testament to the salesperson's prowess and emotional intelligence.

As we peel back the layers of commission-based sales, it becomes clear that it's not just a job—it's a lifestyle. It shapes one's approach to risk, reward, and personal development. It's a crucible where character is forged, and only those with a blend of grit, charisma, and strategic acumen rise to the top.

In conclusion, the psychology of commission-based sales is a rich tapestry of human behavior and motivation. It's a realm where the thrill of potential gain dances with the specter of risk, where the sweet taste of success is savored all the more for the challenges overcome to achieve it. For those who can master its nuances, commission-based sales are not just a means to earn a living; it's a pathway to a 'Next Level Life.'

Financial Planning for Sales Professionals

Embarking on a commission-based career in sales can be likened to setting sail on the vast, unpredictable ocean of market demand. Your financial stability is tethered to the ebb and flow of sales successes and the occasional droughts of client interest. To thrive, you must craft a vessel sturdy enough to weather these fluctuations—a robust financial plan. This guide is your compass to creating that plan, ensuring that when the sales winds are favorable, you are poised to capture the breeze, and when they're not, you remain steadfast and secure.

Your ultimate destination is financial resilience—a state where you can maintain your lifestyle regardless of the natural variance in your income. This means building a safety net that allows you to absorb periods of low income without sinking into debt or distress. Picture your life with a financial buffer that cushions the impact of market downturns and economic storms. It's about creating a life where your finances serve your well-being, not vice versa.

Before we chart your course, you'll need to gather some essential tools:

1. A detailed record of your monthly income and expenses.
2. A clear understanding of your fixed versus variable costs.
3. Access financial planning tools, software, or a trusted financial advisor.
4. A commitment to disciplined saving and spending habits.
5. Knowledge of investment strategies suitable for your risk tolerance and goals.

Your financial plan should encapsulate several key phases:

1. Assessment of your current financial situation.
2. Definition of short-term and long-term financial goals.
3. Creation of a budget tailored to a fluctuating income.
4. Establishment of an emergency fund.
5. Exploration of investment opportunities to grow your wealth.
6. Regularly review and adjust your financial plan.

Let's delve deeper into each phase, ensuring no stone is left unturned.

1. Start by scrutinizing your financial statements. How does money flow in and out of your life? When are peak earning times, and when do things typically slow down? Identifying patterns helps anticipate future trends.

2. Determine what you're aiming for. Do you want to buy a home, save for retirement, or fund your children's education? Establish clear, measurable goals for each milestone.

3. Craft a budget that accounts for the irregularity of your income. Base your spending on your average income, not your best month. This ensures you're not overcommitting financially during leaner times.

4. Aim to save at least three to six months' worth of living expenses. This fund is your financial lifeboat, offering peace of mind and security when sales are slow.

5. Invest in diversified assets to build wealth over time. Consider low-cost index funds, real estate, or other vehicles that match your risk tolerance.

6. Revisit your financial plan at least semi-annually. Adjust your strategies to align with income, expenses, and life circumstances changes.

   - Automate your savings to ensure consistency.

   - Cut unnecessary expenses to maximize your savings rate.

   - Seek professional advice to optimize your tax situation.

   - Avoid high-interest debt; it can quickly become a salesperson's quicksand.

   - Don't rely on a future windfall; base your financial decisions on the present.

   - Be wary of investment schemes promising quick returns; they often carry high risk.

How do you know if your financial plan is seaworthy? It should enable you to live comfortably without incurring debt during low sales periods. You should also see your savings and investments steadily grow over time. If you can handle unexpected expenses without panic, that's a strong indicator of a solid plan.

Should you hit an unexpected financial snag, don't despair. Revisit your budget and cut back on non-essential spending. Consider temporary side gigs to bolster your income. Tap into your emergency fund—but only as a last resort.

Financial planning for sales professionals isn't just about managing money; it's about steering your entire life toward stability and success. With each step outlined in this guide, you're not only preparing for the unpredictability of sales but also paving the path to a 'Next Level Life.'

In this journey, remember: the calm sea never made a skilled sailor. Your ability to plan and adapt financially will distinguish you from the rest, enabling you to sail through the toughest storms and bask in the glory of the most radiant days. Embrace the challenge and let the adventure of financial planning begin.

Cultivating a Positive Attitude

In the tumultuous world of sales, where the only constant is change, the power of a positive attitude cannot be overstated. The beacon guides you through the fog of uncertainty, the wind propels you forward when the waters are still. A positive attitude Is not just a transient state of mind; it's a way of life, a strategic asset in your sales arsenal. With this mindset, we delve into the concept of maintaining positivity amidst the innate unpredictability of the sales profession.

Understanding the power of positivity starts with recognizing its impact on your daily activities. It influences how you approach challenges, interact with clients, and, ultimately, how you close deals. Positivity is not about ignoring the reality of difficult situations; it's about approaching them with a mindset that seeks solutions and opportunities for growth. It's the difference between seeing a failed pitch as a setback or as a learning experience that hones your skills for the next opportunity.

Consider the story of Steven, a seasoned sales executive known for his unfailing optimism. Steven didn't dwell on the loss, even when a major deal fell through after months of negotiations. Instead, he gathered his team, acknowledged their hard work, and focused on the lessons learned. He believed every 'no' brought them closer to a 'yes.' Steven's attitude kept morale high and encouraged a culture of resilience. His team surpassed their sales targets, a testament to the power of a positive outlook.

Let's look at it from different perspectives. A cynic might argue that positivity is a form of naiveté that glosses over reality. However, research in the field of positive psychology presents a counterargument. Studies show positive emotions broaden our sense of possibility and open our minds to more options. Sales professionals are more likely to recognize diverse opportunities and develop creative solutions when they maintain a positive attitude.

Data also supports the notion that positivity can lead to better sales outcomes. A study by the University of Pennsylvania found that optimistic salespeople outsell their pessimistic counterparts by up to 37 percent. This isn't merely a coincidence; it reflects how a positive mindset attracts clients and fosters trust, leading to more successful transactions.

Of course, the concept of positivity can seem nebulous without a concrete understanding of its components. Terms like 'optimism,' 'resilience,' and 'grit' are often thrown around, but what do they truly mean? Optimism refers to the expectation of good outcomes, resilience is the ability to recover quickly from difficulties, and grit is the passion and perseverance for long-term goals. Each of these qualities can be cultivated and is critical for maintaining a positive attitude in sales.

As we distill the essence of this discussion, remember the key takeaways. A positive attitude in sales is not just about feeling good; it's about actively shaping your reality to foster success. It's about leveraging optimism to fuel persistence, using resilience to bounce back from setbacks, and applying grit to achieve your long-term objectives. By cultivating a positive attitude, you're not just improving your sales performance; you're elevating your entire life to the next level.

Ultimately, selling is as much about your mindset as it is about your skill set. The challenges and uncertainties are inevitable, but your response to them is a choice. Choose positivity and watch as it transforms not only your sales results but also the quality of your life. As you close this chapter, ask yourself: How can I apply a positive attitude to my next sales challenge? The answer to this question might be the key to unlocking your 'Next Level Selling' and, consequently, your 'Next Level Life.'

Risk-Taking and Reward in Sales

In an ever-shifting landscape of commission-based sales, the high stakes of risk and reward beckon with the allure of opulent spoils for the victorious yet conceal treacherous pitfalls for the unwary. Thriving in such a capricious environment demands courage and the acumen to discern when to leap into the fray and watch from the sidelines. But what happens when the tightrope of decision making stretches out before you, fraught with potential windfalls and calamities?

The primary issue at hand is the balancing act between taking calculated risks and securing consistent rewards. The seductive promise of a lucrative deal often tempts sales professionals, but this siren call can lead to perilous waters. The consequences of misjudging these risks are not trivial; they can result in lost time, depleted resources, and even a tarnished reputation.

Picture a sales landscape where professionals recklessly chase every lead without a strategic plan, no matter how dubious. The result would be akin to a gambler relying on luck rather than skill— a recipe for disaster. The fallout from such an approach can be severe, with a domino effect of lost clients, diminished earnings, and a beleaguered spirit.

But amidst this uncertainty, a solution emerges, gleaming with the promise of equilibrium. The method lies in fine-tuning the art of risk assessment. By developing a keen eye for evaluating the potential of each opportunity and weighing it against possible downsides, sales professionals can navigate these tumultuous waters with greater confidence.

Implementing such a solution begins with education. A thorough understanding of market trends, client needs, and the nuances of each product or service is paramount. Armed with knowledge, a salesperson can then craft a risk matrix—a tool to visually parse out high-reward prospects from those fraught with excessive danger.

Imagine a sales team deploying this matrix, each member poised with a map of potential outcomes. They proceed with precision, their decisions backed by the clarity of data and analysis. The results speak for themselves: a portfolio of successful deals, a reputation for shrewd judgment, and a steady ascent in earnings.

While this approach has proven its merit, considering alternatives is prudent. Some advocate for a more intuitive method, relying on gut feelings honed by years of experience. Others suggest diversifying broadly, spreading risks across many ventures, much like a sailor setting multiple nets to increase the catch.

Yet, in the realm of sales, as in life, no strategy is foolproof. The key is to find a balance that aligns with one's risk threshold and aspirations for reward. To bolster this quest, one might draw inspiration from the tales of seasoned sales veterans who have weathered storms and basked in the sun's glory. These narratives are not mere anecdotes; they embody lessons learned in the crucible of experience.

Consider, for a moment, the story of Elena, a sales maven who, through meticulous risk analysis, turned an uncertain venture into a resounding triumph. Her approach was not born of reckless abandon but of a measured stride, taking one calculated step after another. Her success was not a stroke of fortune but the fruit of strategy and sagacity.

Now, let us look deeper. How do you, the intrepid sales professional, discern the opportune moment to strike? What tools will you wield to untangle the Gordian knot of risk and reward? These questions beckon with the promise of mastery over the fickle tides of sales.

Ultimately, it is not merely about the risks taken or the rewards reaped. It is about transforming your approach to sales—and, by extension, life. It is about elevating your practice to an art form, where every decision is a brush stroke on the canvas of your career.

As you ponder the path ahead, consider this: What risk, if taken today, could become the cornerstone of your success tomorrow? The answer to this question might catapult your earnings to new heights and redefine your conception of 'Next Level Selling' and 'Next Level Life.'

Success Stories: Commission-Based Champions

On a crisp autumn morning, the conference room was abuzz with anticipation. Eager faces were turned towards the podium, where a lone figure stood with a commanding presence. It was none other than James Larson, a legend in the world of commission-based sales. The room was filled with up-and-comers, each hungry for the secret recipe that transformed ordinary salespeople into extraordinary success stories.

James began with a tale that seemed more like an adventure than a sales pitch. "It was a Wednesday like any other," he said, the timbre of his voice painting the scene, "but by sunset, I'd made the biggest sale of my career." The audience leaned in, hanging on his every word. He wasn't just narrating his victory; he was reliving it. His eyes sparkled with the fire of that moment, and everyone in the room could feel the heat.

Every detail James shared was meticulous, from the nervous tapping of his pen before the call to the triumphant slam of his car door as he drove home that evening. But it was the emotional undercurrent that captivated the audience. He spoke of the fear of rejection, the weight of the mortgage sitting on his shoulders, and the relentless drive that pushed him to dial one more number, to knock on one more door.

Then came the twist. The client seemed a sure bet and was on the brink of backing out. The unexpected obstacle threw James off his rhythm, but this very challenge unearthed his true potential. He took a breath, regrouped, and with a blend of empathy and expertise, he turned the tide, securing a sale and a loyal client for years to come.

This story wasn't just about triumph against the odds; it touched on a deeper truth that resonated with everyone in the room. It was about the transformative power of resilience, which can turn a faltering campaign into a landmark success. James's journey was a microcosm of what every commission-based salesperson faces: the highs and lows, the doubts and the breakthroughs.

As he concluded his anecdote, James promised the audience that they could tap into this wellspring of tenacity and skill. "Each obstacle you face," he said, "is an opportunity to rise above and redefine the boundaries of your potential. The stories you'll hear today are not just mine to tell; they are mirrors in which you'll see your future selves."

In that room, filled with the shared pulse of ambition, James's words were more than pep talk; they were a beacon, guiding the way to next-level selling and, with it, a next-level life.

Have you ever stood at the edge of a decision that feels as daunting as it is vital? Have you felt the tremor of uncertainty ripple through you, wondering if you have what it takes to leap? Let me tell you, you are not alone. Every champion you admire once stood where you stand now.

Take Sophia Ramirez, for example. A single mother of two, juggling life's demands with a grace that belied her struggles. Her entry into commission-based sales was not a calculated career move but a necessity born from a dire situation. Yet, within her story, we find the essence of harnessing adversity and transforming it into an engine of success.

Sophia's early days were fraught with challenges. Clients were skeptical, leads were scarce, and the shadow of doubt loomed large. But she kept refining her approach with each setback, learning from each 'no' until the 'yeses' began to flow. Her success was not an overnight sensation, but a tapestry woven from persistence and passion.

Picture Sophia now, a top-tier sales director, her name synonymous with innovation and excellence. How did she cross that chasm from struggle to stardom? Was it simply a matter of time, or was there a defining moment that changed everything? It was, in fact, a bit of both. A key insight that shifted her perspective, coupled with the unyielding drive that fueled her ascent.

The tales of James and Sophia are but two among countless narratives of those who have conquered the realm of commission-based sales. Their stories are not outliers; they are beacons, shining a light on the path that lies ahead for you. As you turn each page, you will uncover the strategies, the mindset shifts, and the indefatigable spirit that define Commission-Based Champions.

So, ask yourself, what's your story going to be? What heights will you reach when you embrace the principles laid out in these pages? Imagine a future where your name resonates in conference rooms, where your story ignites the spark in others.

You are on the cusp of something great. The journey may be arduous, but the rewards are unparalleled. Embrace the challenge, for in the crucible of commission-based sales; you will not only forge a career but also craft a life marked by excellence and fulfillment.

Remember, every master was once a disaster. Every champion was once a contender who refused to give up. So, what will you do with the lessons from these champions? How will you write the next chapter of your story?

Let's take this journey together. Let's elevate our selling to levels we've only dreamed of and, in doing so, elevate our lives to heights we've never before imagined.

Building a Support Network

Imagine standing at the precipice of your next great sales achievement, feeling the rush of potential coursing through your veins. But as you gaze into the expanse of opportunity, a sobering thought emerges: no one succeeds in a vacuum. The towering sales figures, like the James Larsons and Sophia Ramirezes of the world, didn't reach their summits solo. They built robust support networks, scaffolding that elevated them through the unpredictable terrain of commission-based sales. This chapter is your blueprint for constructing a similar foundation that will hold you steady during tumultuous times and propel you to new heights.

The objective here is clear: to create a vibrant, multifaceted network of allies, mentors, peers, and professionals who can offer advice, encouragement, and resources as you navigate your sales journey. The building blocks for this network are as essential as they are diverse, ranging from industry connections to personal confidantes.

Before we delve into the fabric of this network, let's lay out the necessary materials. You'll need a willingness to reach out, humility to seek guidance, and the foresight to recognize the value in every relationship. A well-maintained contact list is crucial, as are strong communication skills and a genuine desire to foster reciprocal relationships.

Now, let's briefly overview what establishing such a network entails. You'll begin by identifying potential members and then move on to cultivating these relationships. You'll learn how to leverage these connections for mutual benefit, maintain them through consistent engagement, and utilize them as a sounding board for strategies and ideas.

The first detailed step is to identify who should be in your network. Look for individuals who are successful and willing to share their knowledge. These can include experienced salespeople, industry experts, trainers, coaches, and even clients who have shown a vested interest in your professional growth. Remember, diversity in your network is strength—each person brings a unique perspective and set of skills.

Next, you must cultivate these relationships with care. Reach out with a personal touch, perhaps commenting on a recent success they've shared or an article they've published. Networking events, both in-person and virtual, offer fertile ground for planting the seeds of these connections. Be sure to follow up with a message expressing your genuine interest in what they do and how you might support each other.

Practical advice for strengthening these ties is simple yet profound: be as interested in giving as you are in receiving. Offer your skills and insights generously. Be the connector who introduces people within your network to each other, thereby creating additional value. A word of caution: avoid transactional networking. Aim for authentic connections rather than a mere exchange of favors.

To test the strength of your network, periodically ask for feedback on ideas or for help in solving a problem. The responsiveness and quality of advice you receive will indicate how well your network functions.

Don't be discouraged if you encounter a lack of engagement or discover that a connection isn't as beneficial as anticipated.

Troubleshooting these issues can be as simple as revisiting your approach. Perhaps you need to offer more value or clarify your needs. Sometimes, it's necessary to prune your network, focusing on the relationships that are truly reciprocal.

Envision your network as a living, breathing entity. It requires care and attention to flourish. Imagine the stories you'll share, the victories you'll celebrate together, and the challenges you'll help each other overcome.

So, what will your first step be? Will you contact that admired industry leader you've been following on LinkedIn? Maybe it's time to engage more deeply with your peers, finding common ground and shared aspirations.

Your journey in commission-based sales is not a solitary one.

With each connection you forge and every piece of advice you give and receive, you're not just building a network; you're constructing the framework of your future success.

Your Next Level Selling is more than tactics and techniques; it's about the people who will stand by you, guide you, and cheer for you. It's about the lives you'll touch and the ones that will, in turn, enrich yours. This is more than a career; it's a tapestry of relationships that will define your Next Level Life.

Remember, the strength of your sales is directly proportional to the strength of your support network. Today is the perfect day to begin weaving this essential safety net. So, take that step, reach out, connect, and watch as your Next Level Selling transforms into your Next Level Life.

The Fear Factor: Turning Anxiety Into Achievement

Fear is an ever-present companion. It whispers doubts during cold calls, plants anxiety before pitches, and casts shadows over closing deals. But what if this fear, often perceived as a foe, could be reimagined as a friend? What if the very thing that holds us back could launch us forward?

The common issue here is fear, a powerful, often paralyzing emotion every sales professional encounters. It's the chill down your spine when you dial the number of a potential big client. It's the trembling of your hands as you prepare to ask for a sale. Fear in sales is pervasive; it's a primal reaction to the risk of rejection, failure, or the unknown.

Left unchecked, fear can have devastating consequences. It can erode confidence, stifle growth, and ultimately derail careers. Salespeople who cannot master their fear often lock themselves in a cycle of missed opportunities and regret.

But there is a transformation waiting to unfold. The solution? Harnessing fear as a driving force for sales success. This approach doesn't seek to eliminate fear but to channel it, turn the tables, and use it to our advantage.

To implement this strategy, we must first understand the roots of our fears. Is it a lack of preparation? Is it the daunting specter of past failures? Identifying the source is akin to a doctor diagnosing an illness; only then can the proper treatment begin.

Once we've pinpointed the cause, we can start the process of reframing. This involves changing our internal dialogue from one of self-doubt to one of self-empowerment. Instead of thinking, "What if I fail?" we challenge ourselves with, "What if I succeed?" It's about recognizing that fear is not a barrier but a powerful motivator, a sign that we are stepping out of our comfort zones where growth happens.

Preparation is the next critical step. Fear starts to lose its grip as we arm ourselves with knowledge about our products, clients, and market. We develop scripts for cold calling, role-play various selling scenarios, and practice our pitches until they feel second nature. With each rehearsal, the looming figure of fear shrinks, replaced by a growing sense of competence and readiness.

Now, consider the evidence supporting this approach. Look at the top performers in any sales organization, and you'll often find individuals who have learned to channel their fear into focus. They are the ones who see each call as a challenge to be met, each rejection as a step closer to yes. Their achievements are not despite their fears but because they have learned to use them as fuel.

While this method is impactful, it's not the only way to tackle fear in sales. Some professionals find solace in mindfulness and meditation, techniques that help calm the mind and reduce anxiety. Others may opt for professional coaching or therapy to uncover and address deeper psychological barriers. These alternatives are valuable and can be used in conjunction with the principles of fear transformation.

Imagine you're about to enter a high-pressure sales meeting. Your heart races, palms sweat, the familiar signs of fear. But this time, you smile. You recognize these sensations for what they truly are: signs that you're ready, care, and on the edge of something great. This is your moment to shine.

What will your next move be? Will you allow fear to dictate your actions, or will you consciously embrace it, to let it propel you toward your goals? Your choice could redefine your career, transforming your anxieties into the milestones of your success story.

Your Next Level Selling is not a journey free from fear but one where fear becomes a catalyst for growth and achievement. It's about overcoming, not avoiding. This isn't just a career; it's an adventure in self-discovery, resilience, and triumph.

So, as you turn the page on old fears and step into a new chapter of courage, remember that the greatest achievements often lie just beyond the reach of our fears. It's time to harness your fear, make it your ally, and unlock the door to your Next Level Life.

CHAPTER 10

LEADING BY EXAMPLE:
THE SALES LEADER'S GUIDE

The Qualities of an Effective Sales Leader

I n the ever-evolving landscape of business, the helm of any successful sales team is an effective sales leader. As we embark on this new chapter, it is crucial to understand the traits that define such leaders and empower them to drive their teams to unprecedented heights.

Let us begin by outlining the key characteristics we will explore—traits that, when woven into the very fabric of a leader's persona, can propel a sales team to achieve remarkable success.

- Visionary Insight
- Empathetic Engagement
- Unwavering Resilience
- Strategic Agility

- Inspirational Communication
- Integrity and Accountability
- Data-Driven Decision-Making

Visionary Insight

A sales leader's ability to see beyond the horizon sets the stage for future triumphs. Visionary insight is not merely about predicting trends but creating a compelling picture of the future that ignites a collective drive towards a common goal. Such leaders harness the power of foresight to steer their ship through uncharted waters, often before their competitors even realize there is a new ocean to explore.

Evidence of this can be seen in the stories of industry pioneers who, through their foresight, have disrupted markets and created new paradigms. Steve Jobs, for instance, envisioned the potential of the personal computer and, later, the smartphone—foreseeing and shaping the needs and desires of consumers before they themselves recognized them.

In practice, visionary leaders use this insight to develop innovative sales strategies, anticipate customer needs, and guide their teams through changes confidently and clearly.

Empathetic Engagement

The heartbeat of sales leadership is empathy. An empathetic leader listens intently, understands deeply, and connects genuinely with both customers and team members. This emotional intelligence fosters a culture of trust and openness, where team members feel valued, and customers feel understood.

Research in the field of psychology reinforces the impact of empathy in leadership—showing that empathetic leaders are more successful in building rapport and long-term relationships. It is this connection that transforms a transaction into a meaningful interaction.

Practical applications are evident in customer interactions where an empathetic approach leads to stronger relationships and customer loyalty. Empathy also plays a pivotal role in coaching sales team members, helping them overcome challenges and grow.

Unwavering Resilience

The path of sales is laden with rejections and setbacks. Resilience is the armor a sales leader wears to withstand the barrage and emerge stronger with each blow. This quality enables leaders to maintain a positive outlook and steady course, even in the face of adversity.

Consider the experience of a seasoned sales leader who encountered a significant loss in revenue due to an unexpected market shift. Rather than succumb to defeat, they used the setback as a learning opportunity, adjusting their strategy and rallying their team towards a recovery that ultimately led to a stronger market position.

Resilient leaders model this behavior, teaching their teams to view failures as stepping stones rather than stumbling blocks.

Strategic Agility

The landscape of sales is dynamic, with change being the only constant. Leaders who exhibit strategic agility can pivot and adapt their strategies swiftly and effectively. This agility is rooted in a deep understanding of the market and the team's unique strengths.

One can see strategic agility in action when a sudden change in the competitive landscape requires an immediate response. A leader with agility can quickly reassess the situation, align resources, and execute a new strategy to capitalize on the change.

Inspirational Communication

A leader's words can either spark a fire of motivation or smother the embers of potential. Inspirational communication is about crafting messages that resonate, motivate, and call to action. It's not just what is said but how it's said that can turn a routine meeting into a rallying cry for success.

As the legendary motivational speaker Zig Ziglar once said, "People often say that motivation doesn't last. Well, neither does bathing—that's why we recommend it daily." The best sales leaders live by this adage, continuously fueling their team's drive with compelling narratives that inspire peak performance.

Influential leaders employ storytelling as a powerful tool to connect, engage, and inspire their teams, painting vivid pictures of success and the path to achieve it.

Integrity and Accountability

The foundation of lasting leadership is built upon the bedrock of integrity and accountability. A leader who embodies these principles earns their team's unwavering respect and loyalty. They set the standard for ethical behavior and take ownership of successes and failures.

In the realm of sales, where the pressure to hit targets can sometimes lead to ethical gray areas, a leader's commitment to integrity is paramount. It guides their actions and sets a clear moral compass for their team to follow.

Leaders who prioritize accountability create an environment where team members learn to take responsibility for their actions, leading to a culture of continuous improvement and trust.

Data-Driven Decision-Making

In the information age, the ability to synthesize data into actionable insights is a game-changer. Influential sales leaders use data to inform their decisions, removing guesswork and enhancing the precision of their strategies.

By leveraging analytics, a sales leader can identify trends, measure the effectiveness of sales tactics, and make informed decisions that drive better results. The use of data is a testament to a leader's commitment to objectivity and continuous improvement.

Consider how a sales leader might dissect conversion rates and sales cycle lengths to fine-tune their team's approach, resulting in more efficient processes and increased sales.

In conclusion, the tapestry of an effective sales leader is woven with threads of visionary insight, empathy, resilience, agility, inspiration, integrity, and data-driven acumen. These qualities, when combined, form a leader capable of elevating their team to the 'Next Level' in both selling and life. As we delve deeper into each trait, remember this: leadership is not a destination but a journey—a continuous quest for growth, excellence, and impact.

Coaching for Sales Excellence

Embarking on pursuing sales excellence is akin to setting sail on a vast and unpredictable ocean. The goal is clear: to chart a course that will lead your team, with you at the helm, to the shores of unparalleled success. The journey will be demanding, but the rewards are as substantial as they are gratifying. You are about to learn how to elevate your team's sales skills and performance to unprecedented levels, guiding them towards mastery of their craft and, consequently, a more fulfilling professional life.

The objective, the lighthouse guiding your efforts, is to transform your sales team into a powerhouse of skill, strategy, and success. By the end of this journey, you will have instilled in your team the ability to engage customers confidently, navigate objections with finesse, and close deals with a proficiency that speaks volumes of their training and your leadership.

Before setting sail, make certain you have all you need for the voyage:

1. A comprehensive understanding of your product or service.

2. Insight into your target market and customer personas.

3. Access to sales data and performance metrics.

4. A suite of sales tools and technologies at your disposal.

5. A commitment to ongoing learning and development.

6. An open channel of communication within your team.

Imagine the entire process as a map spread before you. At the outset, you'll evaluate your team's current capabilities and identify areas for growth. Following this, you'll tailor a coaching program that addresses these areas through targeted training, practical exercises, and real-world application. Regular feedback and performance analysis will ensure that your team stays on course, while encouragement and recognition will serve to motivate and inspire.

Picture your team as a set of intricate gears in a finely-tuned machine; each member's success is integral to the overall performance. Begin by assessing individual strengths and weaknesses through a mix of self-evaluation and performance data analysis.

From here, design a personalized coaching plan that includes:

- Skill-building workshops focused on areas like communication, negotiation, and time management.

- Role-playing scenarios that simulate challenging sales situations.

- Sales calls and meetings co-led by you or a seasoned team member to provide live, hands-on experience.

- Regular one-on-one check-ins to discuss progress, set goals, and address concerns.

As you coach your team, keep these pearls of wisdom in mind:

- Be patient. Excellence is not achieved overnight.
- Celebrate small victories. They pave the way for larger ones.
- Encourage a collaborative spirit. Sales is not a solo sport.
- Beware of burnout. Balance rigor with recognition.

How will you recognize when your team has reached a new tier of sales excellence? Look for these signs:

- A consistent increase in sales figures and conversion rates.
- Positive feedback from customers about their buying experience.
- A noticeable improvement in team morale and engagement.
- A reduction in turnover, as team members feel more competent and appreciated.

If progress stalls consider these remedies:

- Revisit your coaching plan. Is it tailored to your team's needs?
- Encourage peer-to-peer learning. Sometimes, a colleague can offer the most relatable advice.
- Introduce new sales tools or resources that might invigorate your team's approach.

With your map laid out and your compass set, you are ready to guide your team through the treacherous waters of the sales world. Remember, the journey to sales excellence is just as much about the transformation of your team as it is about the numbers they produce. Under your guidance, they will achieve their sales goals and embark on a path to a more rewarding and impactful career, which is, after all, the essence of a 'Next Level Life.'

Creating a Culture of Sales Success

The atmosphere within which your team operates can either be a springboard to unprecedented heights or a quicksand pit that stifles progress and ambition. The culture of your sales department is not just an invisible backdrop; it's the air your team breathes, shaping their attitudes, behaviors, and, ultimately, their success. But what happens when this culture is found wanting when it fails to inspire or drive your team toward the objectives you've so meticulously outlined?

Imagine a garden where the soil is left unattended, where weeds are given free rein to choke the burgeoning plants. This is akin to a sales environment lacking a culture of success, where short-term pressures eclipse long-term growth, competition overshadows collaboration, and fear of failure paralyzes potential. The consequences of such an environment are grave; diminished morale, high turnover rates, and a tarnished brand reputation are just a few of the perils lurking in the shadows of an undernourished sales culture.

Now, consider the transformative power of a garden tended with care, where each plant is nurtured according to its needs, where the soil is rich with nutrients, and where every weed is promptly removed. This embodies a thriving sales culture that cultivates excellence, encourages resilience, and celebrates success. But how does one foster such an environment?

The solution lies in a multifaceted approach that begins with leadership. As a sales leader, you must become the gardener, meticulously tending to the culture of your domain. It starts with setting a vision that resonates with every team member, aligning them toward a common purpose. This vision must be more than a target; it must be a calling that ignites passion and dedication.

To bring this vision to life, you must sow the seeds of a positive mindset, cultivate a sense of ownership, and prune any behaviors that threaten the culture you desire to grow. This involves recognizing and rewarding efforts, not just outcomes, and establishing a system where feedback is constructive, timely, and, most importantly, a two-way street.

Implementing such a cultural transformation requires concrete steps. Begin by clearly communicating your vision and the values that underpin it. Involve your team in this process; let their voices be heard and their insights considered. This inclusion fosters a sense of belonging and investment in the culture you're building together.

Training and development programs should be tailored to reinforce your established cultural values. Whether it's through regular workshops, peer mentoring, or professional development courses, ensure that growth and learning are not merely encouraged but embedded in the routine of your sales force.

Moreover, cultivate an environment where risks are taken, and failures are viewed as stepping stones to mastery. Celebrate the lessons learned from a lost sale as much as the triumph of a deal closed. This shifts the focus from fear of failure to a growth mindset that values experimentation and innovation.

Evidence of the success of such cultural shifts can be found in organizations that have prioritized their internal environment. These companies often boast higher employee engagement, increased customer satisfaction, and superior financial performance. The correlation is clear; a culture that champions growth and achievement in sales is a potent driver of overall success.

While robust, this approach is not the only way to cultivate a successful sales culture. Some organizations might succeed in fostering hyper-competitive environments or adopting a more laissez-faire attitude that gives salespeople free rein. However, such alternatives often come with their own set of challenges and may not be sustainable in the long run.

As a sales leader, you must steward your team by transforming your sales culture. It is a journey that requires patience, strategic thinking, and a steadfast commitment to your values. Embrace this challenge with the knowledge that the culture you cultivate within your sales team can become the cornerstone of their professional success and their fulfillment. After all, a career in sales is more than a job; it's an opportunity for continuous growth, learning, and achieving a next-level life.

And so, as you turn the pages of this guide, ask yourself: What kind of culture do I want to cultivate? What legacy do I wish to leave within the walls of this organization? The answers to these questions will be the compass that guides your efforts, the wind that fills your sails, and the beacon that lights your way to creating a culture of sales success.

Motivating Your Sales Team

The vitality of your sales team hinges on their motivation, a force that can lead to stunning triumphs or, if absent, to untold setbacks. The key to unlocking the full potential of your team lies in the artful blend of inspiration and practicality. As we dig into the pulsating heart of sales team motivation, we shall explore various strategies designed to keep your team driven and laser-focused on their objectives.

In the subsequent sections, we will uncover a collection of powerful strategies that can elevate your team's performance and morale. This inventory serves as a beacon, illuminating the path to a next-level sales dynamic and, consequently, a next-level life for each team member.

The strategies we will explore include:

1. Personalized Incentive Programs
2. Mastery and Progression Opportunities
3. Constructive Feedback Systems
4. Recognition and Rewards
5. Team Building and Camaraderie
6. Work-Life Balance Initiatives

Incentives are the fuel that can accelerate your team's engine, but not all fuel is created equal. To truly motivate, incentives must resonate on a personal level.

Personalized incentive programs consider each team member's unique motivations and aspirations. Whether it's a monetary bonus, additional vacation time, or professional development opportunities, tailoring incentives ensure relevance and effectiveness.

Companies like Google and Zappos have long been praised for their customized approach to incentives, and they report higher levels of employee satisfaction and performance as a result.

Implement a system where team members can choose their rewards within a framework. This empowers them to work towards something that has personal significance, thereby driving their ambition and productivity.

Growth is a fundamental human need; the sales domain is no exception.

You instill a sense of forward momentum by providing clear pathways for advancement and skill development. Mastery and progression opportunities encourage continuous learning and honing one's craft.

According to a report by LinkedIn Learning, 94% of employees would stay at a company longer if it invested in their career development.

Create mentorship programs and offer workshops and courses that align with your team's career trajectories. This not only boosts their skills but also their loyalty to the company.

Feedback is the compass that guides improvement, but its delivery is a delicate art.

Constructive feedback systems are designed to provide regular, actionable insights that help team members understand their performance and areas for growth without deflating their morale.

A study by Gallup found that employees who receive regular feedback feel more engaged and are less likely to leave their jobs.

Establish weekly check-ins and use them as opportunities to celebrate successes and address areas for improvement in a non-confrontational manner.

Regardless of size, every victory is a steppingstone towards greater achievements.

Recognition and rewards for both individual and team successes create a culture of appreciation that fuels further success. It's not just about grand gestures; often, it's the small acknowledgments that resonate most.

Bersin, by Deloitte's research, indicates that companies with recognition programs highly effective at improving employee engagement have 31% lower voluntary turnover.

Implement a 'kudos' system where peers and supervisors can easily acknowledge each other's accomplishments. Celebrate milestones and share success stories in team meetings.

A team unified in spirit is unstoppable.

Team building and camaraderie go beyond occasional outings; they're fostered through everyday interactions and a shared sense of purpose. When team members genuinely enjoy each other's company, collaboration soars.

Studies show that close work friendships boost employee satisfaction by 50%, and those with a best friend at work are seven times more likely to be fully engaged.

Encourage informal social interactions, create cross-functional project teams, and organize events that allow personalities to shine.

Sustained motivation requires more than just professional fulfillment; it demands a harmonious work-life balance.

Work-life balance initiatives recognize that employees have lives outside of the office and that respecting this balance is crucial for long-term motivation and health.

According to the American Psychological Association, work-life balance strategies can reduce stress, lower absenteeism, and higher employee retention.

Offer flexible scheduling, remote work options, and support for family and personal time. This prevents burnout and conveys that you value your team members as whole individuals.

In the intricate dance of motivation, the nuanced understanding of human desires and needs sets apart the exceptional leader. Can you see your team not as cogs in a machine but as vibrant individuals with unique motivations and dreams? Are you ready to harness these strategies and propel your team to new heights? The journey to next-level selling—and a next-level life—begins with the steps outlined in these pages. Embrace them and watch your team soar.

Setting the Pace: The Leader as a Role Model

The leader stands as the helmsman and the beacon, guiding the team through tumultuous waters with a steady hand and a clear vision. Within this role, the leader's behavior, more than any spoken directive, sets the tone for the team's conduct, ambition, and morale. The essence of leadership lies not in the power to command but in the power to inspire, to lead by example, and to set a pace that others aspire to match. Something I learned as a Ranger.

Leadership is more an action than a title; leaders impart their most enduring lessons through actions. For every sales team aiming to ascend to new heights, it is the leader's responsibility to demonstrate what it means to embody the values, work ethic, and dedication necessary for success. This chapter dives into the profound impact a leader's actions can have on the team's performance and overall life satisfaction, both within and beyond the sales floor.

Consider the leader who arrives early, stays late, and approaches each challenge with a solution-oriented mindset. Their dedication is contagious, instilling a culture of commitment and resilience. Conversely, a leader who cuts corners or shows indifference toward their responsibilities sends a message that such behavior is acceptable, if not expected. This is why the leader's every action must be a conscious choice, a testament to the standards they expect their team to uphold.

By sharing real-life anecdotes of leaders who have successfully transformed their teams, we can see the power of leading by example in action. Take, for instance, the story of a sales director who, despite significant market challenges, consistently demonstrated a positive attitude and a relentless pursuit of innovative solutions. This approach kept the team motivated during tough times and fostered an environment where creative thinking thrived, leading to a breakthrough strategy that turned the company's fortunes around.

From a different perspective, consider the leader who recognizes the importance of empathy and emotional intelligence. They understand that their team members are not just sales figures or quotas but individuals with diverse backgrounds and personal struggles. By showing genuine care and support, this leader creates a sense of safety and belonging within the team, which translates into a deeper commitment to the collective goals.

Supporting these narratives are statistics that reinforce the significance of role modeling in leadership. Research indicates that teams led by individuals who "walk the talk" are more cohesive, experience lower turnover rates, and achieve higher overall performance. Moreover, when leaders demonstrate a healthy work life balance, they implicitly allow their team to do the same, leading to decreased burnout and increased job satisfaction.

It is also essential to clarify any industry-specific jargon or complex sales concepts that leaders exemplify. For instance, when discussing CRM (Customer Relationship Management) systems or sales funnel optimization, a leader should explain these tools and visibly utilize them to maximize team performance and efficiency.

As we draw near the conclusion of this discussion, it is paramount to encapsulate the critical takeaways. A leader's actions have a ripple effect, shaping the team's ethos and defining the parameters of what is achievable. To lead is to serve as a living embodiment of the principles and practices that one espouses.

As a leader, are you prepared to scrutinize your behaviors and ensure they align with the high standards you set for your team? Will you accept the mantle of role model, understanding that each decision you make, each word you speak, and each action you take is a building block in the edifice of your team's culture and success?

Next-level selling demands next-level leadership. It is a journey of continuous self-improvement and unwavering dedication to the craft. As you turn the page, remember that the ultimate measure of your leadership is not where you stand in moments of comfort and convenience but where you stand in times of challenge and controversy. It is there, in the crucible of leadership, that you have the opportunity to elevate your selling to unprecedented heights and, in doing so, elevate your life and the lives of those you lead to the next level.

Sales Leadership Case Studies

Leadership is the thread that weaves together a robust and result oriented team. The stage is set within one such team, a microcosm of potential and drive, yet riddled with the complexities of a rapidly changing marketplace. Their story unfolds in the bustling metropolis of New York City, where the skyline is as ambitious as the sales targets set by the corporations that tower over Manhattan.

Here, we meet the main players: a vibrant sales team at the cusp of innovation in the tech industry and their newly appointed leader, Elizabeth Jones, a veritable force with a reputation for turning underperforming teams into top-market contenders. Elizabeth's background as a Silicon Valley prodigy and her subsequent rise through the ranks of corporate leadership have been nothing short of meteoric.

The challenge presented to Elizabeth was multifaceted: rejuvenate a dispirited team, recalibrate their sales strategy to a rapidly evolving tech market, and, crucially, deliver a turnaround in sales numbers that had been declining quarter after quarter. The task at hand was akin to steering a ship through a storm with the added pressure of an expectant crew looking to her for direction.

Elizabeth's approach to this daunting task was both innovative and grounded. She began by instituting a series of one-on-one meetings with each team member, aiming to understand their strengths, motivations, and areas for improvement. Her strategy was clear: build from within to create a robust and resilient sales force. She implemented a mentorship program pairing seasoned employees with new hires, fostering an environment of learning and mutual support.

The results were nothing short of spectacular. Within two quarters, the team's sales had increased by 45%. The office buzzed with a newfound energy, and the sales floor became a breeding ground for innovative selling techniques that combined traditional methods with cutting-edge technology.

Upon analyzing and reflecting on this success, it was evident that Elizabeth's leadership style was the catalyst. Her ability to empathize with her team and insistence on accountability and excellence engendered a sense of collective ownership over the team's goals. She had addressed the surface symptoms of the team's issues and dug deep to uproot the underlying causes of their stagnation.

Visual aids adorned the walls of the sales floor, with charts tracking progress and celebrating milestones. These served as motivational tools and a barometer for the team's success, offering a clear visual narrative of their journey from underperformance to excellence.

Elizabeth's story is emblematic of the larger narrative of transformative sales leadership. It underscores the pivotal role of a leader in not just driving sales but in crafting a culture of success that permeates every aspect of a team's function.

As we segue from this tale of triumph, consider this: What is the measure of true leadership? Is it the ability to meet targets, or does it extend beyond numbers to the essence of team dynamics and individual growth? How can you, as a leader, foster a culture of excellence that meets the marketplace's immediate demands and prepares your team for the challenges of tomorrow?

Innovative Sales Training Techniques

Empowering a sales team in today's fast-paced market demands more than traditional training methods. It calls for a fresh approach that transcends the conventional wisdom of sales strategies and delves into the core of what makes a salesperson truly influential. As we turn the page from the inspiring leadership journey of Elizabeth Jones, we find ourselves at the threshold of a new chapter: Innovative Sales Training Techniques.

This chapter is dedicated to modern sales trainers and managers who are ready to challenge the status quo and equip their teams with the tools necessary for transcendence in both professional and personal realms. The techniques outlined here are not only about selling more; they're about selling better, with integrity, empathy, and a deep understanding of the customer's needs. Let's embark on this transformative journey together.

1. Immersive Role-Playing

2. Data-Driven Sales Analytics Training

3. Mindfulness and Emotional Intelligence Development

4. Gamification of Sales Training

5. Mobile Learning and Microlearning Modules

6. Social Selling Mastery

7. Collaborative Learning Environments

Immersive Role-Playing

Gone are the days of monotonous script recitations. Immersive role-playing is a cutting-edge technique that plunges salespeople into realistic customer interactions. By simulating high-stakes sales scenarios, salespeople can practice and hone their responses to various customer personas and objections in a risk-free environment. The realism of these exercises sharpens their on-the- spot thinking and adaptability, skills critical for success in the field.

Evidence from companies that have adopted immersive role-playing speaks volumes. These organizations have witnessed a marked improvement in their sales team's confidence and a reduction in the time it takes new hires to become proficient. A testimonial from a top-performing sales representative at a leading software company shared, "Immersive role-playing was a game- changer for me. It was like a sales boot camp that prepared me for the unpredictability of real customer interactions."

The practical applications of immersive role-playing are extensive. Sales teams can rehearse product launches, difficult customer negotiations, and cross-selling techniques within various industry-specific contexts. This preparation ensures that when they face such situations in reality, they are well-equipped to navigate them successfully.

Data-Driven Sales Analytics Training

Harnessing the power of data analytics is no longer optional in the sales industry; it's imperative. Training your team to interpret sales data effectively can lead to more informed decisions and strategies. It involves teaching salespeople to analyze patterns, forecast trends, and understand the competitive landscape through the lens of data.

Companies that have invested in data-driven sales analytics training report a significant improvement in target setting and achievement. One sales director noted, "Understanding data has allowed our team to focus on the right leads and optimize our sales process, resulting in a consistent increase in our conversion rates."

By mastering data analytics, sales teams can tailor their approaches to individual customers, predict market changes, and allocate resources more efficiently. These skills are indispensable for any sales professional looking to advance in today's data-rich environment.

Mindfulness and Emotional Intelligence Development

In a profession where stress is often a constant companion, mindfulness and emotional intelligence (EI) can differentiate between success and burnout. Training that focuses on these aspects equips salespeople with the tools to manage their emotions, build better relationships with clients, and approach negotiations with a level head.

Studies have shown that sales professionals with higher levels of EI are more likely to close deals and maintain valuable client relationships. A sales veteran with over two decades of experience shared, "Learning to stay present and manage my emotions helped me navigate complex deals easily and foster long-term client trust."

Practical applications of mindfulness and EI in sales include stress reduction techniques before high-pressure meetings, empathetic communication skills to understand client needs better, and strategies for maintaining composure in the face of rejection or conflict.

Gamification of Sales Training

Gamification transforms the learning process into an engaging and competitive experience. By incorporating elements of play and competition into sales training, learning becomes more interactive and enjoyable, leading to higher retention rates of information.

A major retailer reported a 30% increase in sales after implementing a gamified training program. The program included leaderboards, badges, and rewards to incentivize performance. A sales associate from the company expressed, "The gamification of our training made learning fun and ignited a healthy competitive spirit that drove us to perform better."

The practical application of gamified training includes setting up sales challenges, tracking progress through levels, and offering recognition and rewards for achievements. This approach motivates the sales team and fosters a culture of continuous improvement and excellence.

Mobile Learning and Microlearning Modules

With the rise of remote work and on-the-go lifestyles, mobile learning and microlearning modules have become essential tools for sales training. These bite-sized, focused training sessions can be accessed from anywhere, allowing sales professionals to learn at their own pace and on their schedule.

Companies implementing mobile learning and microlearning have seen an uptick in training participation rates. A regional sales manager stated, "Our team can now fit training into their busy schedules without feeling overwhelmed. It's a flexible and efficient way to stay up-to-date with the latest sales techniques."

Salespeople can use these modules for just-in-time learning, such as brushing up on product knowledge before a client meeting or learning a new sales tool on the fly. This training approach is convenient and aligns with the modern salesperson's need for flexibility and autonomy.

Social Selling Mastery

Social selling—using social media platforms to connect with prospects and build relationships—is no longer a novelty; it's a necessity. Training your team in social selling techniques equips them with the skills to leverage their online presence for sales success. This includes creating valuable content, engaging with potential customers, and building a personal brand that resonates with the target audience.

A B2B company that trained its sales team in social selling techniques reported a 40% increase in leads generated through social media channels. An account executive said, "Social selling has allowed me to reach prospects more personally and effectively. It's about building relationships, not just pushing a product."

The practical applications of social selling include crafting compelling social media profiles, using social listening tools to identify potential leads, and engaging with industry influencers to expand reach. It's a powerful way to humanize the sales process and connect with customers more deeply.

Collaborative Learning Environments

Finally, fostering a collaborative learning environment is key to a thriving sales team. When sales professionals share knowledge, experiences, and strategies, they create a culture of collective growth. Training encouraging collaboration, such as group workshops or peer coaching sessions, can lead to a more cohesive and high-performing team.

Organizations that have embraced collaborative learning have found that their sales teams are more innovative and adaptable. A sales trainer observed, "When our team members learn from each other, they not only gain new insights but also develop a sense of camaraderie that translates into better teamwork and results."

Practical applications of collaborative learning include creating internal forums for knowledge sharing, organizing team-based problem-solving sessions, and fostering mentorship programs where experienced salespeople guide newcomers.

As we navigate these innovative sales training techniques, remember that the ultimate goal is not merely enhancing sales figures. It's about cultivating a team of professionals who excel in their craft and lead fulfilling lives in and out of the office. These techniques are steppingstones on the path to next-level selling and, indeed, a next-level life.

Now, ask yourself: Which of these techniques resonates the most with your vision for your sales team? How can you implement these strategies to meet your sales goals and inspire a lasting impact on your team's professional development and personal well-being? Pursuing excellence in sales is a journey that never truly ends, but with the right training, it's a journey that can be as rewarding as it is successful.

CHAPTER 11

HEALTH AND SALES PERFORMANCE: THE UNSEEN LINK

Nutrition for the Sales Professional

In the high-stakes game of sales, every edge counts. Sharpening your sales acumen and honing your pitch is undoubtedly crucial, but have you considered the fuel that powers your performance? Welcome to "Nutrition for the Sales Professional," where we dig into the dietary choices that can propel you to peak performance and, consequently, a next-level life.

As we embark on this journey, remember that the mind and body are inextricably linked; what nourishes one feeds the other. With a keen focus on this symbiotic relationship, we present a curated list of nutritional strategies tailored for the sales dynamo. This list is not merely a set of guidelines but a foundation for a transformative way of living that aligns with your goals.

The Essentials of Optimal Nutrition:

1. Balanced Macronutrient Intake

2. Hydration: The Silent Sales Weapon

3. Brain-Boosting Foods

4. Timed Eating for Sustained Energy

5. Supplements: The Helping Hand

Balanced Macronutrient Intake

A balanced diet is a cornerstone of sustained energy and focus. Carbohydrates, proteins, and fats are the macronutrients that serve as the primary energy sources for our bodies. But how do they influence a sales professional's day-to-day hustle?

Carbohydrates are the body's preferred energy source. Whole grains, fruits, and vegetables provide the glucose that keeps your brain alert and your conversations engaging. Proteins are the building blocks of neurotransmitters, the chemical messengers that keep your mood buoyant and your mind sharp. Lean meats, legumes, and dairy can be your allies in this respect. Fats, particularly omega-3 fatty acids found in fish, nuts, and seeds, support cognitive function and emotional health.

The evidence supporting a balanced macronutrient intake is overwhelming. Studies reveal that professionals who maintain a balanced diet report higher energy levels and better focus. Testimonials from top sales performers often cite a well-rounded diet as a component of their success.

Practical applications of this knowledge are straightforward: start your day with a breakfast rich in complex carbohydrates and proteins to fuel your morning's endeavors. Opt for a lunch that combines all three macronutrients to avoid the dreaded afternoon slump. A dinner that's lighter on carbohydrates but rich in proteins and healthy fats can ensure you wake up refreshed.

Hydration: The Silent Sales Weapon

The human brain is composed of approximately 75% water. Even mild dehydration can impair cognitive functions, affecting your ability to think critically and respond swiftly. It's no wonder that hydration could be your silent sales weapon. A regular intake of water throughout the day can maintain your mental acuity and physical energy.

Embarking on your sales day without adequate hydration is like riding on a road trip with a half-filled gas tank. You wouldn't take that risk with your car, so why do it with your body? Research indicates that even a 2% drop in body water content can noticeably degrade mental and physical performance.

The practical applications are as clear as a glass of water: keep a bottle at your desk, sip throughout your client meetings, and maybe substitute that third cup of coffee with a refreshing drink of water. Your body and your sales numbers will thank you.

Brain-Boosting Foods

Imagine eating your way to a sharper mind and a more persuasive pitch. Enter brain-boosting foods – a class of nutrients that directly impact brain function. Fatty fish, rich in omega-3 fatty acids, enhances brain health. Antioxidant-packed berries combat oxidative stress, which can affect your cognitive clarity. Dark chocolate, with its flavonoids, caffeine, and antioxidants, offers a trifecta of benefits: mood elevation, focus improvement, and a touch of indulgence.

The proof is in the pudding—or, in this case, the salmon fillet.

Studies show that individuals who regularly consume omega-3-rich foods display improved cognitive function. Sales professionals who have integrated brain-boosting foods into their diets report heightened clarity and an increased ability to navigate complex negotiations.

Incorporate these foods into your meals in imaginative ways. A smoothie with berries, spinach, and a scoop of protein in the morning, a salmon salad for lunch, or a piece of dark chocolate as a mid-afternoon treat can all contribute to a more focused and effective sales approach.

Timed Eating for Sustained Energy

The concept of timed eating isn't just about what you eat but when you eat it. Aligning your mealtimes with your body's natural rhythms can optimize energy levels and cognitive function. Skipping breakfast can leave you sluggish, and eating too close to bedtime can disrupt your sleep.

Evidence from nutritional science confirms that irregular eating patterns can lead to decreased mental acuity and increased stress levels. A sales professional must always be on top of their game, and irregular eating habits can be a significant hindrance.

The practical application is to establish a routine. A hearty breakfast kickstarts your metabolism and primes you for the morning's challenges. A light, protein-rich lunch keeps you alert through the afternoon. A well-timed snack can provide a boost before that end-of-day pitch. Dinner should be satisfying yet not overly heavy, allowing for restful sleep.

Supplements: The Helping Hand

Supplements can serve as a supportive measure in your nutritional arsenal. While they should not replace whole foods, they can fill gaps and provide additional benefits. A multivitamin can safeguard against deficiencies, while specific supplements like B vitamins or magnesium can support energy production and stress management.

A lot of tangible evidence supporting supplements can be found in the experiences of those who use them wisely. A salesperson who travels frequently may not always have access to nutrient-dense meals, and in such cases, supplements can be a lifesaver.

Practical applications involve consulting with a healthcare professional to identify which supplements may benefit you and incorporating them into your daily regimen with a focus on complementing, not replacing, a balanced diet.

Transitions between these nutritional strategies should be seamless and integrated into your lifestyle. A balanced diet, adequate hydration, brain-boosting foods, timed eating, and strategic supplementation can collectively elevate your sales performance and enhance your quality of life. Remember, a well-nourished body fosters a sharp mind, and a sharp mind closes deals.

As you turn the page on poor eating habits, envision the sales professional you will become with the proper fuel in your tank. Your body is the vehicle for your success; nourish it well, and it will take you to the next level in sales and life. I know this to be fact as I do live a next level life with proper nutrition just discussed.

Exercise: A Salesperson's Secret Weapon

We have navigated the terrain of nutrition and its pivotal role in sharpening the mind and fortifying the body for the relentless demands of the sales profession. Now, let us shift our focus to an oft-overlooked ally in the quest for peak professional performance: exercise. When integrated into one's routine, this fundamental activity can dramatically elevate a salesperson's game and, by extension, their life.

The tapestry of a salesperson's day is woven with threads of energy, resilience, and mental agility. However, the wear and tear of this high-pressure career can fray these threads, leading to burnout and decreased productivity. The primary challenge confronting many in the field is maintaining a peak performance level amidst their role's rigors.

Left unchecked, this strain can manifest in a myriad of detrimental ways. Chronic stress, for instance, can cloud judgment and impede decision-making, while a sedentary lifestyle can invite health issues that further erode one's professional edge. The consequences are clear: diminished sales, a tarnished reputation, and a potential downward spiral in career and personal well-being.

But what if there was a keystone habit that could not only counteract these adverse outcomes but propel you towards greater heights? Exercise that's the powerful catalyst we're honing in on. Regular physical activity is a bulwark against the storm, offering benefits directly translating to enhanced sales performance.

What does this entail, practically speaking? A consistent exercise regimen tailored to individual preferences and goals. This could mean starting the day with a brisk run to clear the mind and invigorate the body. Alternatively, It might involve strength training to build the physical resilience that underpins mental fortitude. Or perhaps the centered calmness achieved through yoga can help gracefully navigate the ebb and flow of sales negotiations.

The evidence underscoring the potency of exercise is compelling. Studies have repeatedly shown that individuals who engage in regular physical activity exhibit improved cognitive function, sharper memory, and heightened creativity. These are the tools of the trade for a salesperson, the arsenal that sets the exceptional apart from the average.

Picture this—a salesperson who exercises regularly is likely to be more energetic and alert, exuding confidence that is palpable to clients and colleagues alike. They're able to keep pace with the demands of their schedule, bouncing back from rejections with a resilience forged in the crucible of their workout routine. Their success stories are many, testifying to the transformation exercise can bring about.

But let's not stop there. What about those days when fitting in a full workout seems impossible? Consider alternative solutions such as micro-workouts—short bursts of activity woven throughout the day. These can mitigate the effects of prolonged sitting and keep the metabolism humming.

And let's not forget the power of walking meetings, which can break the monotony of office confines while stimulating both the body and the mind. The result? A sales strategy that is dynamic, engaging, and ultimately more effective. I promise you; teams love this!

Imagine yourself as that salesperson who harnesses the secret weapon of exercise to meet and exceed targets. Visualize the vitality suffusing your every interaction, the mental clarity that sharpens your pitch, the stamina that carries you through marathon negotiation sessions. This is the promise of what lies ahead when you commit to making physical activity a cornerstone of your daily routine.

Could there be a more compelling invitation to action? Consider this: when was the last time you felt genuinely invigorated after a day's work? It can be your everyday reality. As you stand at the crossroads, the path towards a next-level selling approach and a next-level life is clear. Embrace exercise and watch as it propels you toward the zenith of your potential.

Are you ready to rise to the challenge and experience the transformative power of this secret weapon? Step forward, and let the journey begin.

Mental Health and Sales Stress

In the sometimes-chaotic sales world, where every handshake and smile could mean the difference between success and failure, the psychological toll on those who navigate this high-stakes maze is often an unspoken burden. The relentless pursuit of quotas and the constant pressure to outperform not only competitors but also oneself can lead to a precarious tightrope walk over the chasms of stress and anxiety.

The sales environment is fraught with rejection, uncertainty, and the demand for continuous high performance. Amidst this, the primary issue that emerges with striking clarity is the mental health of sales professionals. The culture of 'always be closing' can gradually erode the psychological resilience of even the most seasoned salesperson.

Left to rot, the consequences can be dire. Anxiety and depression, two silent predators lurking in the pressure cooker of sales, can immobilize a once-dynamic sales force. The cost is measured in lost sales and opportunities and the profound impact on a person's quality of life. The fall from grace in the sales leaderboard is not just a professional setback; it can be a personal crisis, often unseen until it reaches a breaking point.

But what if we could construct a robust defense against this onslaught? The solution lies in a proactive approach to mental health, with strategies designed to insulate sales professionals from the psychological strains of their careers.

One such strategy is introducing a comprehensive mental health support system within sales organizations. This could include access to counseling services, regular mental health awareness training, and establishing a culture that encourages open dialogue about mental well-being.

The implementation of this solution requires a multi-faceted approach. Sales leaders must lead the charge by normalizing conversations about mental health and advocating for resources to support their teams. Moreover, sales professionals must adopt self- care techniques, such as mindfulness meditation or cognitive- behavioral strategies, to bolster their mental fortitude.

The projected outcomes are promising. Research suggests that workplaces that prioritize mental health not only see a reduction in absenteeism but also an increase in productivity. Sales teams supported in this way are better equipped to tackle challenges with resilience and maintain high-performance levels without sacrificing their mental well-being.

Is there a one-size-fits-all solution? Certainly not. Some may find solace in peer support groups, where shared experiences foster community and understanding. Others might prefer individual therapy, where personalized strategies to combat stress and anxiety can be developed.

Imagine a sales team where members feel valued for their contributions to the bottom line and overall well-being. Picture a salesperson who, upon feeling the creeping tendrils of stress, knows they have a support system to turn to, tools to help them navigate through the fog, and the assurance that their mental health is a priority. This is the vision we must strive to realize.

The evidence is clear: companies that invest in mental health initiatives report a return of $4 for every dollar spent. But beyond the numbers, the actual value lies in the lives enriched through such interventions, the careers salvaged from the brink of collapse, and the human potential unleashed when the mind is cared for with the same diligence as the sales strategies crafted.

Why, then, would any sales organization not take steps to safeguard the mental health of its most valuable asset—its people? The question hangs in the air, a silent challenge to the status quo.

As the pages of this book turn, let the narrative of 'Next Level Selling - Next Level Life' be about strategies and techniques and building a sustainable career that nurtures the mind as much as it rewards the hustle. At the intersection of mental health and peak performance, it is here that the proper next level of selling—and living—lies.

Ultimately, a sale is not just a transaction; it's the culmination of countless hours of effort, resilience, and often, personal sacrifice. Let's ensure those sacrifices do not come at the cost of our mental health. After all, the most significant sale we can make is selling ourselves on a balanced, healthy life, where success is measured in numbers and the harmony of our professional and personal worlds.

Sleep and Sales: The Performance Connection

As dawn breaks and the world stirs into motion, the ambitious sales professional gears up for yet another day of challenges and opportunities. But before the first email is sent, before the first call is made, a fundamental element has already set the stage for the day's performance: a night of restful sleep—or the lack thereof.

Imagine this: The alarm blares, waking you from a fitful sleep. You recall tossing and turning, the numbers and targets dancing forebodingly in your dreams. As you sit up, the weight of exhaustion hangs heavily on your shoulders, a silent adversary you must now carry through the day. Now, consider the impact of this sluggish start on your ability to sell, connect, and convince.

Herein lies the essence of this chapter: the profound impact of sleep quality on your selling abilities and, by extension, your life.

The claim is straightforward yet powerful: Quality sleep is a critical, though often overlooked, component of sales success. Deprive yourself of it; you might as well be handicapping your potential.

Let's discuss the primary evidence supporting this assertion. Studies have shown that well-rested individuals exhibit enhanced cognitive function, including improved memory, sharper decision-making skills, and greater emotional intelligence—all vital to successful sales interaction. For example, research from the University of Pennsylvania revealed that individuals who slept fewer than six hours a night for two weeks functioned as poorly on cognitive tasks as those who had been awake for 24 consecutive hours.

But let's not just skim the surface. Think about the last time you had a poor night's sleep. Remember the struggle to focus, the irritability, slow comprehension? Amplify that across your sales team, impacting negotiations and client relationships. The evidence is clear—sleep is not just a personal health issue; it's a professional performance multiplier.

Of course, there's counterevidence to consider. Some might argue that high-achieving salespeople often work long hours and get by on minimal sleep, fueled by adrenaline and ambition. They pride themselves on their ability to "burn the midnight oil" and still deliver results.

However, this is where we must rebut with a clarification: Short term bursts of productivity may arise from such habits, but they are not sustainable. The long-term effects of sleep deprivation include burnout, diminished health, and decreased sales performance as cognitive deficits accumulate.

To bolster the initial claim further, let's introduce additional evidence. The Division of Sleep Medicine at Harvard Medical School suggests that chronic sleep deprivation may lead to serious health problems, including obesity, diabetes, cardiovascular disease, and even early mortality—not to mention the toll it takes on mental health, as we've previously discussed.

In conclusion, the assertion that sleep quality directly affects sales performance stands reinforced. Just as an athlete needs rest to perform at their peak, so does a salesperson. To neglect sleep is to neglect the foundation upon which the art of selling is built.

So, I pose a direct question to the reader: Are you giving your sleep the attention it deserves? Or are you letting this performance- enhancing ally slip through your fingers?

As we move forward in 'Next Level Selling - Next Level Life,' let's not forget the integral role sleep plays. It's time to elevate our approach to rest as we elevate our sales strategies. After all, the next level of selling demands a next level of living, and that begins with closing our eyes each night, securing the restorative sleep that our bodies and sales figures so richly deserve.

Work-Life Harmony for Salespeople

In a world perpetually spinning on the axis of high targets and demanding quotas, sales professionals often find themselves caught in a whirlwind of client meetings, negotiations, and relentless pressure to perform. Amidst this daily grind, the delicate scales of work and life tilt precariously, threatening to topple over at the slightest provocation.

The problem is as relentless as it is pervasive: work-life imbalance. It's the silent thief that robs salespeople of their joy, health, and, ultimately, their effectiveness. Left unchecked, this imbalance can lead to chronic stress, deteriorating relationships, and a steep decline in productivity. The consequences are dire— burnout becomes a looming specter, family ties strain, and mental health wavers, casting long shadows over personal and professional landscapes alike.

But what if there was a pathway to equilibrium, a method to meld the demands of selling with the needs of living? This is not a mere possibility but a practical solution that has transformed lives and careers.

The blueprint for balance lies in intentionally structuring time, prioritizing tasks, and setting boundaries that honor professional ambitions and personal well-being. The first step is acknowledgment—recognizing that time is a finite resource and should be allocated judiciously.

Begin by mapping out your week, giving each responsibility its due slot. This includes time for client calls and follow-ups and moments for family, exercise, and leisure. The art of saying 'no' becomes invaluable here; not every request warrants your attention if it infringes on your time.

Next, harness the power of technology to automate routine tasks. Customer relationship management tools can track leads and schedule follow-ups, freeing you to focus on high-value interactions. This boosts your efficiency and carves out precious time for life beyond work.

Implementing these strategies has shown promising results. Salespeople report higher job satisfaction, increased energy for client interactions, and a more joyful engagement with their personal lives. Their testimonials are evidence of the solution's efficacy; they've experienced firsthand the rejuvenation that comes with balance.

Of course, other approaches beckon, promising harmony. Some advocate for strict compartmentalization—balancing work and home life. Others swear by the 'work hard, play hard' philosophy, maintaining that intense work periods should be offset by equally fierce periods of relaxation.

Yet, these alternatives often overlook the subtle interplay between work and life. True harmony is not achieved by swinging from one extreme to the other but by integrating both spheres in a way that complements and enhances each other.

With its myriad hues of obligations and desires, the canvas of your life beckons for a masterful balance. Imagine a life where the close of a successful sale is celebrated with colleagues and loved ones, where the joy of a child's laughter is not a rare treat but a daily blessing.

So, I ask you, do you dare to envision a life where your sales targets are met without sacrificing the moments that make life worth living? Can you commit to the discipline required to achieve this harmony?

As you ponder these questions, remember that the journey to work-life harmony is not a sprint but a marathon. It requires persistence, self-awareness, and a willingness to adapt. But the rewards—enhanced relationships, sustained performance, and a profound sense of fulfillment—are worth the effort.

In pursuing next-level selling and a next-level life, let us not forget the importance of balance. In the grand tapestry of life, it is not just the triumphs on the sales floor but also the joys in the living room that weave the most exquisite patterns. Let this be the guiding principle as we stride forward, seeking success in sales and serenity in life.

The Impact of Substance Abuse on Sales

In the relentless pursuit of success, sales professionals often navigate a labyrinth of stress and expectation. At times, the pressure to outperform can lead to desperate measures, with some turning to the crutch of substance abuse. It is a path that promises fleeting respite but ultimately steers careers and lives off course.

The air in the sales office is thick with ambition, as palpable as the scent of freshly brewed coffee. Each salesperson is a gladiator in their own right, armed with a phone, a contacts list, and a smile that masks a thousand worries. But lurking in the shadow of these daily battles is a silent adversary, one that whispers false promises of enhanced performance and stress relief: substance abuse.

What starts as a means to endure longer hours or to celebrate a closed deal can spiral into relentless dependence. The effects are insidious, creeping up like a shadow at dusk, and before one realizes it, their career, health, and personal life are held ransom by addiction.

Let's paint a picture of the typical consequences. A salesperson reliant on substances may initially feel invincible, buoyed by artificial confidence. However, as reliance deepens, so does the impact on their work. Critical thinking becomes clouded; decision- making is erratic. Clients sense the change; trust, once the bedrock of any sales relationship, erodes. The salesperson's numbers fall, and with them, their spirits.

But imagine an alternative, a lifeline thrown into these troubled waters. The cornerstone of this rescue is a robust support system within the workplace and the personal sphere. Employers can implement programs that encourage healthy lifestyles and offer support for those struggling with substance abuse. Regular training sessions can destigmatize the issue, opening doors to open conversations and assistance.

The implementation phase is as crucial as the solution itself. It requires a dedicated task force that understands the nuances of addiction and can provide tailored support. Employee Assistance Programs (EAPs) are a testament to effectiveness, offering confidential counseling and resources for those in need. The impact of such initiatives can be profound, with studies indicating a significant drop in absenteeism and a boost in productivity among participants.

But what does the evidence suggest about the outcomes of such interventions? A glance at the statistics reveals a promising trend. According to research, comprehensive workplace substance abuse interventions can lead to a 65% reduction in accident rates and a 10% to 30% decrease in absenteeism. These are not just mere numbers; they represent a return to form for many sales professionals, a reclamation of their potential.

Perhaps you're pondering alternatives. Indeed, there are other routes to consider. Some advocate for a zero-tolerance policy, immediate dismissal at the first sign of substance misuse. Others suggest regular mandatory drug testing to keep the salesforce "clean." While these methods may seem straightforward, they often fail to address the root of the problem and can exacerbate the stigma, driving the issue further underground.

Now, pause for a moment. Can you visualize a workplace where success is not measured solely by sales targets but also by the health and well-being of the sales team? A place where a person is guided gently back on track rather than cast aside at the first stumble?

This vision is not a utopian fantasy; it is an attainable reality where compassion and understanding pave the road to recovery. The testimony of those who have walked this road and returned stronger is a beacon of hope. They speak not only of a revived career but of a newfound zest for life, a clarity of purpose that extends beyond the sales floor.

The journey is fraught with challenges in the grand scheme of a sales career. Yet each step taken towards a healthier life, free from the shackles of substance abuse, is a stride towards a next-level selling experience and, indeed, a next-level life.

As we turn the page on this chapter, let us carry with us the knowledge that substance abuse need not be the end of a sales career. Instead, it can mark the beginning of a more authentic, more fulfilling journey in the profession. One where each victory is not clouded by dependency but celebrated with a clear mind and a light heart.

So, as you move forward, ask yourself: Will you be the one to extend a hand to a colleague in need? Will you champion a workplace culture that not only drives sales but also nurtures the well-being of its warriors? The choice is yours, and the impact is immeasurable.

Holistic Health Strategies for Sales Success

The sun rises, casting a golden glow over a new day—a symbol of renewal and the chance to embrace fresh strategies for prosperity. A salesperson steps into the light, equipped with a portfolio of products and the most significant asset at their disposal: their health. Today, we embark on a transformative journey, a roadmap that leads to next-level selling by fostering a next-level life through holistic health strategies for sales success.

The Goal

Our mission is clear: to integrate a holistic approach to health, enabling sustained peak performance in sales. This isn't merely about hitting targets; it's about nurturing the mind, body, and spirit to cultivate resilience, sharpness, and vitality. By the end of this path, you'll be equipped to thrive under pressure and excel in your sales career while enjoying a fulfilling, balanced life.

Necessary Materials or Prerequisites

Before diving into the roadmap, gather the following essentials:

1. Commitment to change and personal growth.

2. Willingness to assess and adapt your current lifestyle.

3. Basic understanding of nutrition, exercise, and mindfulness practices.

4. Access to health and wellness resources like a gym, healthy food, and a supportive community.

5. A journal or app to track progress and reflect on experiences.

Overview:

Our journey unfolds in four strategic phases: Nutrition, Movement, Mindfulness, and Environment. Each step is a pillar, supporting the structure of our greater purpose. Together, they form a holistic fortress, safeguarding our well-being and empowering our sales performance.

Some Detailed Steps:

Nutrition is the fuel that powers our sales engine. Start by overhauling your diet, focusing on whole foods that energize and heal. Incorporate a rainbow of fruits, vegetables, lean proteins, healthy fats, and whole grains. Hydration is vital; drink plenty of water to maintain focus and clarity.

Physical activity is non-negotiable. It's not just about losing weight; it's about building a robust and agile body capable of handling stress. Aim for at least 30 minutes of moderate exercise each day, whether it's a brisk walk, a bike ride, or a dance class. Don't forget to integrate strength training and flexibility exercises to complete your fitness repertoire.

Sales is as much a mental challenge as a physical one. Mindfulness practices like meditation, deep breathing, and yoga can sharpen focus, reduce anxiety, and improve emotional regulation. Dedicate daily to these practices, even just a few minutes. They are the silent guardians of your mental fortitude.

Your environment, both at work and home, should be a sanctuary that supports your holistic health goals. Organize your workspace to reduce clutter and distraction. Surround yourself with plants, natural light, and calming music to enhance concentration. At home, create a restful sleep environment, free of screens and disruptions, to ensure restorative rest.

Some Tips and Warnings:

Throughout this journey, remember the importance of balance. Extreme diets, overtraining, and overzealous meditation can lead to burnout. Listen to your body and mind, adjusting your approach as needed. Consistency trumps intensity: small, sustainable changes are more effective than drastic overhauls.

Testing or Validation:

How will you know you're on the right track? Your sales performance, energy levels, and overall well-being will be the indicators. Reflect on your progress regularly, noting improvements in stamina during long workdays, enhanced clarity during client negotiations, and a more profound sense of calm amidst the chaos.

Troubleshooting (Optional)

If you find yourself slipping back into old habits, don't despair. Revisit your journal, seek support from your community, and remind yourself of your goals. Adjust your strategies as necessary and be patient with yourself. Change is a journey, not a sprint.

In the tapestry of life, each health thread weaves a pattern of success. As you step into your day, remember this: your health is not just a personal asset; it's a professional tool. A vibrant life fuels a thriving career. So, what steps will you take today to ensure your wellness is the foundation of your sales triumphs?

In the grand symphony of sales, let your health be the harmony that elevates your performance. With each client's handshake, with every deal closed, celebrate a professional victory and a personal triumph in your journey towards Next Level Selling and a Next Level Life.

CHAPTER 12

FOLLOW-UP MASTERY:
THE TWO CRUCIAL WORDS IN SALES

The Science of Follow-Up

I n the competitive dance of sales, the spotlight often shines brightest on the grand opening number—the initial pitch. Yet, the true mastery, the art that separates the novice from the virtuoso, lies in a seemingly mundane, often overlooked step: the follow-up.

What exactly is this pivotal maneuver? At its core, the follow- up is the process of re-engaging with a prospect after an initial contact or meeting. It is an opportunity to remind, persuade, and demonstrate value, ensuring that the connection made does not dissolve into the abyss of forgotten interactions.

To dive deeper, the follow-up is not merely a single event, but a series of strategic communications designed to foster a relationship. It is the bridge between a moment of interest and a decision, the nurturing path from potential to actuality. This sequence is akin to the delicate work of a gardener—cultivating, watering, and tending to the seeds of interest until they bloom into the flowers of commitment.

The genesis of this term is not tied to a specific moment in history but has evolved with the practice of trade and negotiation. The concept itself is deeply rooted in the fundamental human need for connection and affirmation, stretching back to ancient marketplaces where merchants would build rapport with customers through repeated interaction.

Positioning the follow-up within a broader context, it becomes clear that it is an essential element of any sales strategy, as it touches upon fundamental psychological principles. The human mind is wired to respond to attention and consistency, which are key components of successful follow-ups. Here, interest is transformed into trust and trust into action.

Imagine a salesperson reaching out to a prospect after an initial meeting with a personalized message that references their conversation. This action serves as a reminder of the product or service and shows that the salesperson is attentive and values the prospect's business. In another instance, a timely follow-up after sending a proposal can provide the nudge for the prospect to review and, perhaps, approve it.

However, the road to mastering the follow-up is littered with misconceptions. One such fallacy is the belief that following up too frequently is bothersome and will push the prospect away. While there is such a thing as excessive contact, consistent and thoughtful follow-up is generally perceived as professional and assertive, not desperate.

The science of follow-up demands finesse. To illustrate, envision a juggler, each ball representing a touchpoint with a prospect. Too few throws and the act becomes dull; too many, and the performance descends into chaos.

But how does one navigate the delicate balance?

Do you ever wonder if your follow-up technique is more akin to a sledgehammer than a feather's touch?

The key is rhythm. In music, rhythm is the thread that binds the notes together into a cohesive melody. In follow-ups, the well-timed sequence of interactions maintains the prospect's interest without overwhelming them. It's about crafting your communications with precision—each word, each message, and each call should serve a purpose and lead the prospect closer to a decision.

Employing vivid imagery, one might compare the follow-up to a carefully choreographed ballet. Each step is intentional, each movement graceful and calculated to complement the music—your sales narrative.

In your follow-up, use language that resonates and reinforces the value proposition. For instance, instead of saying, "Just checking in," you might say, "I've been reflecting on our conversation and how our solutions align perfectly with your goals." This shift in language transforms a mundane check-in into a meaningful reconnection.

Remember, a superb follow-up strategy is not about bombarding your prospects with information but about sparking their imagination and painting a picture of the future where your product or service is integral.

In conclusion, the science of follow-up is about understanding the psychology that drives human interaction and decision-making. It is about recognizing the importance of timing, persistence, and the art of communication. When done right, the follow-up becomes more than a sales tactic; it is the key to unlocking Next Level Selling—and with it, a Next Level Life.

Timing Your Follow-Ups for Maximum Impact

In the intricate dance of sales, where every gesture and step can lead to a triumphant close or a misstep into obscurity, the timing of your follow-up is the essential rhythm that can elevate your performance to a standing ovation. It is your invisible conductor, orchestrating each movement to ensure your message resonates at the perfect moment, capturing attention and sparking decisive action.

Consider the scenario: you've just concluded an exhilarating meeting with a potential client. The air was electric with possibility, the exchange of ideas fluid and promising. But as the days tick by without a word, that initial spark can quickly fade into the background noise of a busy world. The follow-up is your encore, the vital act that can reignite interest and transform it into commitment. But when the timing is off, even the most eloquent of messages can fall on deaf ears.

The challenge here is clear: strike too soon, and you risk appearing overeager or intrusive; delay too long, and you may be forgotten or, worse, replaced by a competitor's timely overture. The consequences of poor follow-up timing are not to be underestimated. A deal that could have blossomed into a lucrative, long-term relationship may wither into a lost opportunity, leaving you to ponder what might have been.

Yet, there is a solution that cuts through the uncertainty, a method that turns the art of follow-up into a science. It begins with understanding your prospect's unique rhythm—when do they review proposals? When are they most receptive to communication? This insight will guide the choreography of your follow-ups, ensuring each touchpoint arrives at a moment when it can have the greatest impact.

To implement this strategy, start with an analysis of past interactions. Look for patterns in response times and consider the context of successful conversions. Did a particular time of day or day of the week yield better results? Use this data to inform your approach, tailoring your follow-up schedule to align with the prospect's habits and preferences.

One might ask, "But how can I know when the time is ripe for re-engagement?" The answer lies in active listening and observation. Throughout your initial meeting, pay close attention to verbal cues or hints about the prospect's schedule and decision-making process. These nuggets of information are the golden threads that will help you weave a follow-up timeline that feels intuitive rather than intrusive.

The proof of this approach's efficacy is not merely anecdotal. Studies in customer relationship management demonstrate that well-timed follow-ups significantly increase the likelihood of a sale. By striking while the iron is hot—when the memory of your meeting is still fresh or when the prospect is in the midst of their decision-making—you elevate your message from background noise to a resonant melody that commands attention.

Of course, there are other schools of thought on follow-up timing. Some advocate for a set interval approach, touching base every few days or weeks. Others suggest a more intuitive style, gauging the prospect's engagement and adjusting accordingly. While these methods have their merits, they lack the precision of a strategy built on the foundation of rhythm and timing.

As you refine your follow-up timing, let your words paint a picture of a shared future where the benefits of your product or service glow brightly against the canvas of your prospect's needs and aspirations. Avoid the dull thud of generic phrases and let your language soar with the vibrant hues of specificity and relevance.

In the final analysis, timing your follow-ups for maximum impact is not merely a tactical decision but a reflection of your dedication to understanding and serving your clients. It is the harmonious blending of persistence and patience, the recognition that each prospect is a unique symphony, and your role is to master its cadence.

By mastering the timing of your follow-ups, you increase your chances of sealing the deal and set the stage for a dynamic, ongoing relationship that can lead to repeat business and referrals. In the meticulous calibration of your follow-up strategy, it is here that you unlock the door to the Next Level!

Personalizing Your Follow-Up Messages

Personalization is the golden key that unlocks the door to deeper connections and more meaningful engagements. When you craft follow-up messages that resonate with each prospect, you're not just sending another email — you're extending a hand for a firm, personalized handshake that can bridge the gap between interest and action, between mere contact and a lasting contract.

Embark on this journey of tailored communication, and you will discover the power of personal touch in transforming your follow-up messages from mere echoes in the digital void to compelling conversations that captivate and convert.

Your mission, should you choose to accept it, is to personalize your follow-up messages so that each one feels like it's been crafted exclusively for the person receiving it. The goal is clear: to demonstrate that you understand your prospect's unique needs, desires, and pain points, thereby increasing the likelihood of progressing the sales conversation toward a successful close.

To embark on this quest, you will need:

- A comprehensive understanding of your prospect's business, industry, and specific challenges.
- Insight into the prospect's personality and communication preferences.
- Access to any previous communication records with the prospect for continuity.

⌨ Creativity to tailor each message while maintaining your brand's voice.

⌨ Patience and attention to detail to ensure each message is fine-tuned to perfection.

The process of personalizing your follow-up communications involves several key steps: gathering information, segmenting your prospects, crafting the message, and then refining it with a personal touch. This overarching strategy ensures that each communication resonates on a personal level.

Firstly, data is your ally, and its thoughtful analysis is your strategy map. Delve into the prospect's business with Sherlockian diligence. What recent successes have they celebrated? What challenges are they grappling with? Have there been any significant changes in their industry? A single golden nugget of information can catalyze a highly engaging message.

Next, consider the prospect's personality. Are they a no-nonsense, just-the-facts individual, or do they appreciate a story woven with wit and warmth? The tone of your message should mirror their communication style. A mismatch could spell the difference between a message that sings and sinks.

Once you've gathered your intelligence, it's time to segment your prospects. Not all customers are created equal, and your messages should reflect that. Categorize your prospects by industry, role, or even by the stage they are at in the buyer's journey, and tailor your messages accordingly.

Now, the artistry begins. Craft your message like a skilled artisan, shaping it with the tools of relevance and specificity. Begin with a strong, relevant subject line — this is the gatekeeper to your prospect's attention. Within the body of your message, reference specific points from your previous interactions or their business to show that you're paying attention and that you care.

A tip to keep in your quiver is the effective use of storytelling. Weave a brief narrative that relates to your prospect's situation, perhaps a success story of a similar client, to demonstrate understanding and potential outcomes.

A word of caution, though: avoid over-familiarity or anything that could be perceived as invasive. You're building a bridge, not breaking down doors. Respect for privacy and professional boundaries is paramount.

How will you know if your personalized messages hit the mark? The responses you receive will be your guide. Increased engagement, more meaningful dialogue, and questions that dig deeper are signs that your messages are resonating. Keep an eye on open rates, click-through rates, and conversion rates to measure the impact of your personalization efforts.

Not every message will be a home run, and that's okay. If you're not getting the responses you hoped for, revisit your prospect's information. Is it accurate and up to date? Consider also soliciting feedback from a colleague or a mentor — sometimes, a fresh pair of eyes can spot opportunities for improvement that you might have missed.

Personalizing your follow-up messages is not just about adding a prospect's name to an email. It's about weaving their world into your words, creating a tapestry of communication that speaks directly to their needs, achievements, and aspirations. It's about showing that you see them not as another name in your CRM but as a real person with goals and challenges that you're eager to help them overcome.

When you send a message that's been carefully personalized, you're not just closing a sale; you're opening a relationship. You're not just pushing a product; you're offering a solution. In the grand narrative of your sales career, these are the moments that stand out — the moments when selling transcends the transactional and becomes truly transformational.

In the following pages, we will continue exploring the strategies that elevate your selling approach. We will dive into the art of active listening, the power of precise questioning, and the mastery of objection handling. Together, these tools will arm you with the prowess needed to reach the next level in selling and craft a next- level life that echoes the rewards of genuine connections and fulfilled potential.

Follow-Up Channels: When to Use Which

The steps you take after the initial contact are as critical as the first impression you make. Your follow-up strategy can mean the difference between forging a lasting relationship and being forgotten. Understanding the various follow-up channels at your disposal and, more importantly, when to use each can help you navigate the complex rhythms of customer engagement with finesse. Let's embark on a journey through the most effective channels, examining their ideal applications to ensure that your message reaches your audience and resonates with them profoundly.

Email: The Swiss Army Knife of Communication

Email remains the quintessential follow-up tool, versatile and widely accepted across industries. Its power lies in its flexibility—you can craft detailed messages with attachments, track opens and clicks, and automate sequences to maintain engagement without constant manual input. However, the secret to email efficacy is timing and personalization. Consider the individual's role and their stage in the buying cycle when crafting your email. Is this a C-level executive who values brevity and high-level insights? Or a technical specialist who might appreciate detailed specs and case studies?

- When using email, provide value in every message. Use information gleaned from initial conversations or social media insights to tailor content. For instance, after a conference, send a follow-up email referencing a topic discussed during a panel that resonated with your prospect's interests.

- Leverage the power of social proof by including testimonials or case studies relevant to the prospect's industry. An email highlighting how your product helped a similar company can be persuasive.

- Employ email tracking tools to gauge engagement and use this data to refine your follow-up strategy. If a prospect frequently opens emails but doesn't respond, it may be time to pick up the phone.

Phone Calls: The Personal Touch

The phone call is a time-honored follow-up channel that offers the immediacy of voice and the nuance of tone, often leading to more dynamic and revealing conversations. Use phone calls when you need immediate feedback or when the subject matter is too complex for written communication.

- Reserve phone calls for moments when personalized interaction can significantly advance the deal. A welltimed call can demonstrate genuine interest and commitment, particularly in resolving concerns or explaining intricate product features.

- Share success stories in a conversational tone, allowing for questions and dialogue. This can help build trust and credibility more personally than written communication.

- A phone call can be the perfect follow-up after a prospect has engaged with several of your emails but hasn't taken the next step. It shows initiative and can often lead to a breakthrough in the sales process.

Social Media: Engaging Informally

Social media platforms provide a casual environment for following up. They can be ideal for maintaining a connection with an active prospect on these channels. However, it's crucial to match the platform to the prospect—for example, LinkedIn for business related follow-ups and Twitter for sharing industry news or insights.

- Use social media to congratulate a prospect on a recent achievement or to share content that aligns with their interests. This can keep the conversation going and reinforce your relationship.

- Share posts from satisfied customers or re-tweet positive reviews of your product. Social proof resonates well on these platforms and can influence prospects more subtly than direct messaging.

- Comment on a prospect's post with valuable insights to demonstrate your industry expertise. This can increase your visibility and credibility, keeping you top-of-mind when the prospect is ready to decide.

Direct Mail: The Tangible Surprise

In an era dominated by digital communication, a piece of direct mail can stand out. Use this channel for high-value prospects where a physical touchpoint could tip the scales in your favor. A well- designed brochure or a handwritten note can make a lasting impression.

- Direct mail should be highly personalized and visually appealing. Use it to send a special offer, an invitation to an exclusive event, or a thoughtful gift that aligns with the prospect's interests.

- Include snippets of customer testimonials within your direct mail piece. This adds a level of trust and can pique the recipient's interest.

- After a significant interaction, such as a product demo, follow up with a thank-you note or a package with additional information. This tangible gesture can enhance the perceived value of your relationship.

In-Person Meetings: The Ultimate Connection

The in-person meeting is the most personal and impactful follow-up channel. Reserve it for high-stakes deals or when a face-to-face conversation could be the deciding factor. The physical presence allows for richer communication, including body language and immediate rapport building.

- In-person meetings should be well-planned and goaloriented. Prepare by reviewing notes from previous interactions and setting clear objectives for the meeting.

- Bring along a portfolio of case studies or arrange for a testimonial from a satisfied customer who can speak to the prospect in person.

- Use in-person meetings to solidify relationships, negotiate final terms, or provide a hands-on demonstration. The investment of time and effort in meeting face-to-face speaks volumes about your commitment to the prospect and the deal.

Navigating between these channels requires a keen understanding of your prospect's preferences and the context of your communication. As you weave through the rich tapestry of follow-up strategies, remember that the ultimate goal is to truly connect on a level that transcends the transaction and cements a partnership. Your sales journey is about reaching targets and building bridges that span industries, personalities, and individual needs. With each follow-up, you're not just pushing a product but fostering a relationship that could flourish into a lifelong connection.

Overcoming Follow-Up Fears

Our journey now takes us into the heart of a pervasive challenge that can stifle progress and dim the bright potential of even the most promising transactions: the fear of following up. As we delve into this realm, we uncover the trepidation that grips many sales professionals—the silent whispers of doubt when it's time to reengage with a prospect. It's a moment fraught with tension, where the fear of being perceived as pushy or bothersome looms large. But what if I told you that these fears, while common, can be conquered with a strategic and empathetic approach?

Imagine the scene: you've made the initial contact, perhaps even conducted a pitch or meeting that seemed to go well, but now the time has come to follow up, and your mind races with uncertainties. Will they view my message as an annoyance? Have they lost interest? These anxieties are not unfounded, for the act of following up is indeed a delicate art.

Let's crystallize the issue at hand. The primary challenge is the fear itself—the anxiety that can cause salespeople to hesitate or even avoid following up altogether. This apprehension stems from a concern about damaging the nascent relationship with the prospect or crossing the line into intrusiveness.

The consequences of succumbing to this fear are significant. Opportunities may slip through your fingers, as a lack of follow-up can easily be interpreted as a lack of interest or professionalism.

Moreover, competitors who are bolder in their approach may swoop in to capture your prospect's attention, leaving you to reflect on what might have been.

However, there is a path forward that can transform this fear into a powerful ally. The solution begins with understanding the psychology of follow-up and embracing a mindset of service rather than intrusion. By approaching follow-up as an opportunity to provide additional value and support to your prospect, you shift the focus from your fears to the benefits you can offer.

Implementation of this solution requires a measured and thoughtful strategy. Start by setting a follow-up schedule that respects the prospect's time. Map out a plan that includes a variety of touchpoints—phone calls, emails, social media engagements, and perhaps even a handwritten note. Each interaction should deliver value, whether it's a piece of relevant content, an answer to a previously unaddressed question, or new insights that could benefit the prospect's business.

Evidence of this approach's efficacy can be found in the stories of those who have mastered the art of follow-up. They report higher conversion rates and deeper, more meaningful relationships with their clients. These salespeople often become trusted advisors, turning single transactions into long-term partnerships.

While the method outlined above is robust, it's prudent to consider alternative solutions. Some sales professionals find success with a more passive approach, such as inviting prospects to subscribe to a newsletter or attend a webinar. This can keep the lines of communication open without the pressure of direct follow- up.

Consider using varied sentence structures to create a dynamic flow in crafting your follow-up communications. Paint a picture of success with vivid imagery, allowing your prospects to envision the positive outcomes of continuing the conversation with you.

Occasionally, pose direct questions that prompt reflection, such as, "Have you considered the impact of X on your current strategy?"

Remember, the use of adverbs and adjectives should be judicious—opt instead for potent verbs and concrete nouns to convey your message with clarity and force. And don't forget the power of a one-line paragraph.

Simple language will ensure your message is accessible, while rhythm and cadence will make your writing more engaging. Where appropriate, weave in quotations or dialogues that lend authenticity to your narrative. And always aim to show, rather than tell, demonstrating through examples and anecdotes the value you bring.

By overcoming the fear of follow-up, you enhance your sales process and enrich your life with the confidence and satisfaction that come from meaningful professional relationships. In the grand tapestry of sales, each thread of connection we weave, undeterred by doubt, strengthens the fabric of our career and adds vibrant color to the canvas of our lives.

Automating Follow-Ups Without Losing the Personal Touch

In the ocean of sales, where the winds of change blow fiercely, and the tides of technology rise unrelentingly, there sails a ship known as 'Follow-Up'. Her crew? Sales professionals who navigate the waves with perfect skill often find themselves adrift when it comes to balancing automation with the human touch. But fear not, for in this chapter, our compass points to a haven where personal connection and automation coexist harmoniously.

Establish the Goal:

Our mission is clear: to harness the power of automation in our sales follow-ups without sacrificing the bespoke charm that makes each prospect feel uniquely valued. Mastery of this art will increase efficiency and fortify the relationships that are the bedrock of successful selling.

Necessary Materials or Prerequisites:

Before embarking on this journey, gather your toolkit: a customer relationship management (CRM) system capable of automation, a collection of personalized templates, insights into your prospects' preferences and behaviors, and a dash of creativity to ensure your communications sparkle with individuality.

Broad Overview:

Picture the journey ahead as a map with various landmarks. Initially, we laid the foundation by setting up automated systems. Next, we personalize our templates, infusing them with life. Then, we schedule follow-ups with precision, and finally, we monitor and adjust our course according to the winds of feedback and data.

Detailed Steps:

1. Setting Up Automated Systems: Begin by integrating your CRM with tools that automate the sending of emails, scheduling of tasks, and logging of interactions. This digital backbone will free you from the mundane, allowing you to devote more time to personalizing your approach.

2. Personalizing Templates: Develop a library of templates for different scenarios—introductions, check-ins, or value propositions. Then, customize them for each prospect, using their name, referencing past conversations, and tailoring your message to their specific needs and pain points.

3. Scheduling Follow-Ups: Use your CRM to create a follow-up cadence that feels natural, not robotic. Factor in the prospect's preferred times for communication and balance automated messages with manual ones.

4. Monitoring and Adjusting: Keep a vigilant eye on the performance of your automated follow-ups. Use metrics

like open rates and response rates to gauge effectiveness and tweak your approach accordingly.

Some Tips and Warnings:

A word for the wise: automation should be a tool, not a crutch. Use it to enhance interaction, not replace it. Be wary of over-automation, which can leave prospects cold. Personal touches, like acknowledging a recent event in their life or referencing a shared interest, can transform an automated message into a personal note.

Testing or Validation:

You'll know you've struck the right balance when your response rates remain steady or improve, and the feedback from prospects is positive. Keep an ear to the ground—sometimes, the most valuable insights come from casual remarks during a call or a quick note in an email.

Troubleshooting:

If you encounter radio silence or a drop in engagement, revisit your automation settings. Perhaps your timing is off, or your messages are too generic. Don't hesitate to pick up the phone for a truly personal touch; it can reset the tone of your relationship.

As the sun sets on this chapter, envision yourself not as a mere salesperson but as a maestro, orchestrating a symphony of followups that resonate with the rhythm of personal care and the efficiency of automation. With each note struck in perfect harmony, your sales and life ascend to unparalleled heights.

Real Follow-Up Success Stories

In the heart of New York City, amidst the ceaseless hum of commerce and the relentless pursuit of success, a sales professional named Susan once found herself on the brink of a career-defining deal. The city's towering skyline was not just a backdrop to her daily routine but a reminder of the heights she aimed to reach. Her prospect, an influential tech firm, was as elusive as it was promising, and months of emails, phone calls, and meetings had led her to a pivotal moment—a moment that could either be her greatest triumph or yet another entry in her ledger of learning experiences.

But this story isn't just about Susan or the techniques she learned from her mentor. It's about how the relentless pursuit of a goal, armed with a strategic follow-up plan, can lead to unexpected success that transcends the bottom line.

Susan's journey with the tech firm began with optimism but soon encountered the inertia of corporate indecision. Her contacts were always cordial, yet their noncommittal responses left her proposals in limbo. Months passed, and Susan felt she spoke into the void with each follow-up.

Yet, she persisted.

As the city wrapped itself in the glamour of upcoming holidays one cold November evening, Susan drafted another follow-up email. This time, though, she infused it with personal stories of clients who had benefitted from her services, painting a picture of the future she saw for the tech firm. She referenced shared experiences, like the time they had to reschedule a meeting due to a city-wide power outage and how they had both laughed about the unpredictability of life in the Big Apple.

And then, something changed.

The next morning brought a response that was different from all the rest. "Your timing couldn't have been better," the email read. It turned out that a competitor's slip-up had just opened a door that Susan's persistent follow-ups had kept her foot in. The tech firm was ready to talk serious business.

In the span of a few weeks, Susan's dedication turned into a closed deal. This deal skyrocketed her career and secured a lasting relationship with a major player in the tech industry. Her story became a beacon for her colleagues, a testament to the power of following up with strategy and heart.

As readers and aspirants of 'Next Level Selling - Next Level Life,' what can we learn from Susan's story?

First, sales is often a long game that requires patience, resilience, and an unwavering belief in the value you bring to the table. Second, personalization in follow-ups can make all the difference, transforming a standard sales pitch into a compelling narrative that captures the attention of even the most elusive prospects.

And third, even in a world where instant gratification is the norm, there is still room for the kind of strategic tenacity that waits for the right moment to strike.

So, what does this mean for you? It means that whether you're a seasoned sales veteran or a greenhorn just starting, the principles of effective follow-up are universal. They can be applied across industries and be the difference between a mediocre career and one that is truly next level.

As you turn the pages of this book, know that the insights and strategies you'll uncover are more than just theories—they are the keys to unlocking a life where success is not just about closing a sale but about creating a legacy of relationships built on trust, persistence, and a deep understanding of the human element in every transaction.

Are you ready to transform your follow-ups into stories of success? Let Susan's story be your inspiration, and let the following pages guide you to the next level of selling—and living.

CHAPTER 13

THE PROSPECT'S ROLE: A REASSESSMENT

Prospect Empowerment Strategies

In the bustling sales world, a quiet revolution brews—shifting the paradigm from seller-driven monologues to a harmonious dialogue where prospects claim their rightful place at the heart of the process. This new chapter heralds an era where empowerment isn't just a buzzword but the cornerstone of a successful sales strategy.

Imagine walking into a room where the air is thick with anticipation, the stakes are high, and every participant is hanging on to your every word. Yet, something is amiss. Despite your best efforts, there's a palpable disconnect, a rift that no amount of persuasive prowess seems to bridge. The problem, as clear as day, is that the prospects feel like passive bystanders in their journey.

They're hungry for involvement, empowerment, and a sense of agency that traditional sales dynamics often fail to provide.

Left unaddressed, this disconnect festers, leading to a cascade of consequences. Engagement plummets as prospects retreat into the shadows of the sales process, their voices muted, their concerns unaddressed. The fallout is tangible—deals stall, conversions dwindle, and a trail of what-ifs lingers long after the final handshake.

But what if the solution lies in redefining the very fabric of the sales encounter? What if, by empowering prospects, we unlock a level of engagement and commitment that transforms the sales landscape? The answer is a resounding 'yes,' and the pathway to such an outcome is paved with strategies that place the prospect in the driver's seat of their decision-making process.

We begin by equipping prospects with knowledge to sow the seeds of empowerment. Knowledge is power; in the sales context, this means providing them with all the information they need to make an informed decision. This includes transparent insights into the product or service, its benefits, and how it stacks up against the competition. Armed with this information, a prospect can engage actively and confidently in the sales dialogue.

Implementation of this knowledge-first approach starts with a comprehensive audit of your communication materials. Assess every touchpoint—brochures, presentations, website content—for clarity and completeness. Are you withholding or overloading information? Strike a balance that informs without overwhelming, ensuring the material is accessible and easy to digest.

Evidence of the approach's efficacy is found in case studies where prospects, transformed into knowledgeable partners, become champions of the product or service. They negotiate not just on price but on value, and their testimonials carry the weight of genuine conviction.

While knowledge is a powerful tool, it is not the only arrow in the quiver of empowerment. Alternative solutions include fostering a collaborative environment where feedback is encouraged and acted upon. Consider creating interactive platforms inviting prospects to share their thoughts and participate in developing the solution they're being sold.

Picture a scenario where a prospect's suggestion catalyzes a new feature or service enhancement. Such co-creation cements the prospect's commitment to the product and elevates their experience from transactional to transformational.

Of course, these strategies require a delicate touch. Their implementation must be as artful as it is strategic. Begin with questions that probe beneath the surface and invite the prospect to envision the future with your solution in hand. "How do you see this fitting into your long-term goals?" Such queries signal genuine interest and empower prospects to articulate their aspirations.

Remember to use adverbs and adjectives like the seasoning in a gourmet dish—just enough to enhance, never to overpower. The potency of your message lies in the strength of your nouns and verbs, the building blocks that convey action and substance.

And when the moment calls for emphasis, do not relinquish the power of a well-placed one-line paragraph.

It's about partnership.

In the dance of dialogue, let rhythm and cadence be your guide. Craft sentences that ebb and flow, mirroring the natural cadence of conversation. And as you weave this tapestry of words, sprinkle in quotations that add authenticity and relatability.

"Empowerment leads to ownership, and ownership leads to success," remarks a seasoned sales director, encapsulating the ethos of this approach.

Lastly, remember the most compelling narratives are those that show, not tell. Paint pictures with your words; let anecdotes and examples breathe life into the abstract, transforming concepts into concrete realities that prospects can see, feel, and believe in.

With these strategies, 'Next Level Selling' becomes more than a title—it becomes a reality where every sales interaction is a step towards a 'Next Level Life' for both you and your prospects.

Shifting From Salesperson to Consultant

In the world of modern sales, an evolution is unfolding—one that beckons sales professionals to ascend from the traditional role of salesperson to the esteemed position of consultant. This transformative journey is not merely a change in title but a fundamental shift in mindset and approach, heralding a new paradigm where trust, expertise, and tailored solutions become the hallmarks of success.

To fully embrace this transition, one must first grasp the essence of the terminology that underpins it. Understanding these terms is akin to deciphering a map that guides one through the intricate landscape of consultative selling.

At the heart of this transformation are several pivotal terms: 'Consultative Selling,' 'Value Proposition,' 'Trusted Advisor,' 'Solution Selling,' and 'Client-Centric Approach.' These concepts are buzzwords and beacons that lead to a deeper connection with clients and a more rewarding sales experience.

Consultative Selling is an approach that prioritizes the client's needs above all. It's a method where the salesperson, now a consultant, delves deeply into the client's challenges and goals. Imagine a doctor diagnosing a patient before prescribing medicine. Similarly, a sales consultant thoroughly analyzes the client's business to offer solutions that are not just products but remedies for business pain points.

A Value Proposition is the promise of the value to be delivered. It's a clear statement that explains how a product or service solves a problem improves a situation or delivers specific benefits. Think of it as an elevator pitch encapsulating the unique advantages of what's being offered.

The term Trusted Advisor reflects the status earned when a sales consultant becomes a key resource for their client. Earning this title is like becoming a confidant to a monarch—the client trusts the consultant to provide strategic advice that can influence crucial business decisions.

Solution Selling shifts the focus from selling a product to selling a solution to a problem. This approach requires a deep dive into the client's issues, fostering an environment where the sales consultant is seen as an architect, and constructing a bespoke solution that fits the unique blueprint of the client's needs.

A Client-Centric Approach is one that revolves around the client's perspective. It's like the North Star for the sales consultant—guiding every decision, interaction, and strategy with the aim of delivering maximum value to the client.

To breathe life into these terms, let us tether them to the familiar. Consider a tailor fashioning a bespoke suit. Each measurement is taken precisely, and the fabric complements the wearer's style and needs. This is the essence of consultative selling—tailoring solutions that fit the client as perfectly as a custom suit.

Now, picture a bridge spanning a vast chasm. The value proposition is that bridge, connecting the client's needs to the solutions offered. It's sturdy, built on the foundations of understanding and benefits that can withstand the weight of client expectations.

Envision a lighthouse standing resilient against a stormy sea, guiding ships safely to the harbor. This symbolizes the role of a trusted advisor, providing direction and security amidst the turbulent waters of business challenges.

Solution Selling is akin to a chef crafting a meal to suit a guest's dietary restrictions. It's a thoughtful process that considers the specific needs and creates a safe and delightful dish.

Finally, adopting a Client-Centric Approach is like a novelist crafting a narrative that resonates with readers. Every plot twist and character is developed with the reader in mind, ensuring the story entertains and connects personally.

These definitions are not mere abstractions but the scaffolding upon which consultative selling is built. They guide the sales consultant in forging a path that leads to enduring relationships and sustained success. By internalizing these concepts, the sales consultant steps into a role that transcends the transactional and enters the realm of partnership and growth.

In this journey from salesperson to consultant, it is not enough to understand the terms; one must embody them. It is a process that demands dedication, insight, and a relentless commitment to the client's success. Through this transformation, the sales landscape is redefined, and the potential for both personal and professional fulfillment is boundless.

The metamorphosis from salesperson to consultant is not a destination but a continuous journey of learning, adapting, and serving. It is the essence of 'Next Level Selling,' a pursuit that elevates the sales professional, the life they lead, and the clients they serve.

The Art of Collaborative Selling

The concept of Collaborative Selling emerges as the golden thread, binding the relationship between seller and buyer with strength and mutual benefit. As we draw the curtains on our exploration of 'Next Level Selling - Next Level Life,' let us dive deep into the heart of what makes Collaborative Selling.

Introduce the Subject:

Collaborative Selling is the dance of synergy where sales professionals and customers move in harmony, creating value together. It's a partnership where dialogue, transparency, and shared goals replace the traditional pitch-and-wait approach. This final chapter is an ode to the power of collaboration, a celebration of its potential to redefine the sales process and enrich the lives it touches.

The Concept:

Imagine a world where the barriers between seller and buyer crumble, giving way to a landscape where both parties work as allies. Collaborative Selling is the embodiment of this vision. It is where the sales professional and the client co-create solutions, leveraging each other's knowledge, experience, and insights. In this realm, the sales process is not a battleground but a fertile ground for ideas, innovation, and growth.

Examples and Illustrations:

Consider a software company working with a retailer to develop a custom inventory management system. The salesperson brings technical expertise, while the retailer offers an in-depth understanding of their operations. Together, they design a system that is effective and uniquely suited to the retailer's specific challenges and goals. This is Collaborative Selling in action – a testament to the power of partnership.

Different Perspectives:

Some may challenge the feasibility of such close cooperation, citing competitive secrets or the fear of over-commitment. However, the success stories of Collaborative Selling are numerous and growing. They demonstrate that when trust is the foundation and the focus is on shared success, the results can surpass even the most optimistic expectations.

Data and Facts:

Studies have shown that collaborative approaches can lead to a 50% reduction in the sales cycle and a significant increase in customer satisfaction and loyalty. This is hard evidence of the tangible benefits that Collaborative Selling brings – benefits that ripple out to touch not just immediate sales targets but the broader ecosystem of business relationships.

Complex Terms:

The term 'Collaborative Selling' may sound intricate, but its essence is simply about working together for mutual success. It's about replacing "us versus them" with "we." It removes the opacity from the sales process, replacing it with a transparent and inclusive approach that values and nurtures the client's voice.

Key Takeaways:

As we conclude, remember that Collaborative Selling is more than a methodology; it's a mindset. It calls for empathy, patience, and a genuine commitment to understanding and fulfilling the client's needs. The key takeaways of this approach are clear: increased trust, deeper relationships, and a synergistic path to success that benefits all.

The essence of Collaborative Selling, and indeed of 'Next Level Selling - Next Level Life,' is the recognition that when we elevate our approach to sales, we promote our relationships, businesses, and ultimately, our lives. It is the way forward, a blueprint for success that is both sustainable and fulfilling. As we turn the last page of this book, let us carry on the lessons learned, the strategies developed, and the spirit of collaboration that can transform our professional landscapes and enrich our journeys.

Remember, in the art of Selling, as in life, the next level is not just about elevating our tactics but our connections and humanity.

This is the true art of collaborative Selling – paving the way for a next-level life.

Building Long-Term Prospect Relationships

In the ever-evolving world of sales, the focus shifts from the immediacy of closing deals to the visionary art of cultivating relationships. "Next Level Selling - Next Level Life" is not just a mantra but a strategic blueprint for sales professionals who aspire to achieve their targets and build a legacy of trust and loyalty with their prospects. In this chapter titled "Building Long-Term Prospective Relationships," we delve into the essence of enduring connections, guiding you through a journey that transcends the transactional to lay the foundations for a mutually prosperous future.

Establish the Goal:

Your destination is clear: creating a network of prospects who believe in you, trust your expertise, and see you as more than just a salesperson but a reliable partner in their growth journey. The goal is to transform prospects into long-term clients who will turn to you repeatedly because they value the relationship beyond your products or services.

List the Necessary Materials or Prerequisites:

To embark on this journey, you will need a few key tools at your disposal:

- Deep knowledge of your product or service
- Insight into your prospect's industry, business, and individual challenges
- Active listening skills
- Patience and perseverance
- Genuine interest in your prospect's success
- Personal integrity and professionalism

Begin with a Broad Overview:

The roadmap to building long-term prospect relationships unfolds in several stages – from initial contact to ongoing nurturing. You will identify prospects, engage with them, understand their needs, provide value, maintain contact, and continuously fortify the relationship.

Dive into Detailed Steps:

1. Identifying Prospects: Start by understanding who your ideal prospects are. Research their business, their challenges, and how your offerings can address their pain points.

2. Initial Engagement: Reach out with personalized communication. Aim to initiate a dialogue that is more about them and less about you.

3. Discovery: Listen more than you talk. Unearth what your prospects truly need, not just what they say they want.

4. Provide Value: Once you understand their needs, demonstrate how your product or service can make a tangible difference. Offer insights, not just information.

5. Follow-up: Keep the lines of communication open. Regularly check in with valuable content, updates, and a genuine question about how they're doing.

6. Strengthen the Bond: Invest in the relationship by celebrating their successes, offering help during challenges, and being present beyond the sales cycle.

Tips and Warnings:

- Be authentic. People can sense insincerity from a mile away.
- Don't rush. Building relationships takes time.
- Always provide value in every interaction. This doesn't mean constant selling; it means being a resource.

⁜ Listen for cues about personal interests and use these to connect on a human level.

Testing or Validation:

You'll know you've succeeded in building a long-term relationship when your prospect:

⁜ Sees you as a trusted advisor, not just a vendor

⁜ Comes to you for advice, even when it's not directly related to a sale

⁜ Refers other potential clients to you

⁜ Offers unsolicited positive feedback about your partnership

Troubleshooting:

If you find the relationship is not progressing, reassess your approach. Are you truly listening? Are you offering solutions to their problems or just pushing a product? Adjust your strategy to be more consultative and focused on their success.

In a sea of transactions, stand out as a beacon of relationships. Picture yourself not as a salesperson but as a trusted ally in your prospect's corner, someone they can count on in a world rife with fleeting connections. As you employ these strategies, you elevate your professional life and enrich your world with lasting, meaningful interactions and bonds.

Now, imagine you've followed this path, and a once casual prospect has now become a cornerstone client, regularly engaging with you and looking forward to your calls. How does that feel? How does it impact your confidence, approach to new prospects, and vision for the future? Reflect on these questions as you progress to 'Next Level Selling - Next Level Life.'

Prospect Feedback: Learning and Growing

Embarking on a journey of sales mastery, you have learned to cultivate valuable relationships that stand the test of time. Yet, the path to excellence is paved with the experiences of success and feedback. In this chapter, "Prospect Feedback: Learning and Growing," we explore the transformative power of feedback from those who matter most in your sales process – your prospects.

Your mission is to harness the insights gleaned from prospect feedback to refine your sales tactics, enhance your professional growth, and, by extension, enrich your life with a deeper understanding of your client's needs and preferences.

Before you begin, ensure you have the following:

- A robust system for collecting feedback from prospects
- An open mind, ready for constructive criticism
- A commitment to ongoing improvement
- Tools for analyzing feedback effectively
- A resilient attitude towards rejection and negative feedback

Take a moment to visualize the cycle of feedback: a continuous loop that starts with listening leads to learning, and results in leveling up your sales game.

Delve into the cycle by dissecting each phase:

1. Collecting Feedback: Create a structured approach to gather comments from prospects, whether it's through surveys, direct conversations, or observation of their responses to your pitches.

2. Analyzing Feedback: Sift through the feedback to identify patterns, commonalities, and anomalies. Differentiate between subjective opinions and constructive insights.

3. Adapting Your Approach: Integrate valuable feedback into your sales strategy. This may involve tweaking your

pitch, adjusting your follow-up routine, or even reevaluating the solutions you offer.

4. Implementing Changes: Put the refined strategies into action. Test them in real-time to experience their impact.

5. Reassessing and Evolving: After implementation, seek out more feedback to gauge the effectiveness of your changes.

As you navigate these steps, consider these tips and warnings:

- Listen more than you defend. Feedback is a golden learning opportunity, not a battleground for your ego.

- Not all feedback is equal. Weigh the feedback against your knowledge and experience.

- Change can be uncomfortable but necessary for growth. Embrace it.

To validate your successful feedback integration, look for improved engagement from prospects, a higher conversion rate, or a more efficient sales process. These are the markers of real progress.

Should you encounter resistance or find that changes are not yielding the desired results, do not despair. Troubleshooting is a part of the process. Revisit the feedback, seek clarification if needed, and be willing to iterate on your strategy.

Now, let the power of feedback transform your interactions. Imagine a scenario where a previously indifferent prospect now reacts positively to your refined approach. This is the fruit of your labor – a testament to your willingness to learn and grow.

As you forge ahead, remember that each piece of feedback is a steppingstone to a higher level of selling and living. Your commitment to this process elevates your professional prowess and enriches your life's tapestry with lessons learned and wisdom gained.

So, ask yourself: What feedback have I been avoiding? How can it propel me toward the next level? Take these questions to heart as you build a life and career that thrives on listening, adapting, and excelling.

Navigating Prospect Resistance

Navigating the choppy waters of prospect resistance is as crucial as a sailor's mastery of the sea. Resistance is as inevitable as the rise and fall of the tides; it can either be a force that capsizes your efforts or one that you adeptly sail through, reaching the shores of success.

Imagine a scenario where you've honed your pitch to perfection, only to be met with a wall of skepticism or disinterest from your prospect. What do you do when your well-crafted messages are met with objections or indifference? The answers lie not in the resistance but in your response.

Prospect resistance, in its many forms, is the primary obstacle every salesperson must overcome to close a deal. The problem is not just the existence of resistance; it's the inability of many to anticipate, understand, and dismantle it. When not properly addressed, resistance can erode trust and stifle the relationship- building that is central to sales success.

The consequences of unaddressed resistance are significant. Deals may fall through, sales cycles can drag on indefinitely, and the rapport you've worked so hard to build can crumble instantly. Prospects might spread their negative experiences with your approach, leading to a tarnished reputation and lost future opportunities.

But fear not, for every challenge bears the seed of opportunity. The solution to overcoming resistance lies in a multi-faceted approach that begins with empathy and ends with a handshake.

First, empathize with your prospects. Place yourself in their shoes to understand the root of their hesitations. Is it a lack of trust, insufficient information, or perhaps past experiences that color their perception? Whatever the reason, empathy is your guide to navigating these murky waters.

Next, tailor your communication to address their specific concerns. This isn't about overwhelming them with facts but about providing targeted information that addresses their needs and alleviates their fears. Your message should resonate with their unique situation, making it clear that you're not just selling a product or service but offering a solution to their problem.

Implementing this empathetic approach requires active listening, patience, and a genuine desire to help. When you encounter resistance, ask probing questions. "What concerns do you have?" or "Can you tell me more about your hesitation?" These inquiries open the door to a deeper understanding and demonstrate that you value their perspective.

As you gather this information, use it to refine your pitch. Perhaps they need testimonials to trust the efficacy of your solution. Maybe a live demonstration or trial period would dispel their doubts. Whatever the case, your ability to adapt your strategy to their needs is paramount.

Evidence of this approach's efficacy is abundant. Sales professionals who practice active listening and empathy report higher conversion rates and more enduring client relationships. They're the ones who don't just meet quotas; they build a loyal customer base that serves as a wellspring for referrals and repeat business.

Of course, there are alternative methods to tackle resistance.

Some salespeople might opt for a more aggressive approach, countering objections with a barrage of facts and figures or discounts. While these tactics may sometimes work, they often serve as a temporary fix rather than a long-term solution. They may win the battle but lose the war, as they do not foster the same level of trust and partnership.

Ultimately, your goal is not merely to sell but to transform a skeptical prospect into a satisfied customer. This transformation is the art of next-level selling, where each interaction is not just a transaction but a step toward a more fulfilling and successful life— for both you and your client.

So, what will you do when faced with resistance? Will you allow it to derail your efforts, or will you embrace it as an opportunity to deepen your understanding of your prospects and refine your sales approach? The choice is yours.

The Prospect's Journey: A Case Study Analysis

The sales landscape is an ever-evolving terrain, and within its bounds, a prospect's journey from curiosity to commitment is fraught with countless decisions and interactions. My personal experiences as a global sales expert and a former U.S. Army Airborne Ranger have taught me that each engagement with a prospect is not just a step in the sales process but a pivotal moment that could redefine their life and, by extension, my own.

Let us look into a case study that exemplifies the nuanced dance between seller and buyer, where strategy, psychology, and human connection converge to turn a challenge into triumph.

Our story unfolds against the vibrant backdrop of the fast-paced tech industry. A revolutionary software platform designed to streamline project management for remote teams had hit a plateau in its market penetration. Despite its innovative features and proven benefits, the sales team struggled to convert interested leads into paying customers.

The central figures in this saga were Emily, a seasoned sales representative with an analytical mind and warm demeanor, and Thomas, a potential client and the CEO of a burgeoning remote marketing agency. Thomas had expressed interest in the software but was hesitant to commit, citing budget constraints and uncertainty about its integration with existing tools.

As Emily quickly identified, the core challenge was not merely financial but rooted in a deeper resistance to change and the fear of disrupting Thomas's team's workflow. To address this, Emily needed a strategy that transcended conventional sales pitches; she needed to weave a narrative that resonated with Thomas's vision for his company and allayed his fears.

Emily approached the solution with a blend of empathy and expertise. She initiated a series of in-depth conversations with Thomas to understand his long-term goals and current operational challenges. Through active listening and pointed questions, Emily painted a vivid picture of a future where the software saved time and resources and empowered Thomas's team to achieve greater innovation and collaboration.

Visual aids played a crucial role in this unfolding story. Emily used flowcharts and testimonials to demonstrate the software's impact on similar companies, highlighting the ease of integration and the long-term cost savings. The data was compelling, but it was the stories of transformation that truly captured Thomas's imagination.

The results? A complete turnaround. Within three months of implementing the software, Thomas's agency reported a 25% increase in productivity and a significant reduction in project delivery times. The initial resistance had given way to enthusiastic adoption as the team discovered new levels of efficiency and job satisfaction.

Reflecting on this case, it becomes clear that the success was not solely due to the software's features. Emily's ability to listen, understand, and articulate a vision aligned with the client's needs. However, one must also consider potential criticisms: Could the outcome have been different if the agency was less adaptable?

Was the sales strategy too reliant on the prospect's openness to change?

Connecting this case study to the larger narrative of 'Next Level Selling - Next Level Life,' we see the universal truth that selling is not about the product or service itself but the transformation it enables in the customer's life. It's about guiding prospects through their journey with a steady hand and an open heart.

CHAPTER 14

CREATING YOUR OWN LUCK IN SALES

Preparation Meets Opportunity

In the bustling world of sales, serendipity is often mistaken for mere coincidence, a lucky break that falls into the lap of the fortunate few. But what if I told you that these so-called strokes of luck are not as random as they seem? What if the key to unlocking these moments lies within our grasp?

Let's talk about a concept that is foundational not just to selling but to life itself: preparation meets opportunity. In its simplest form, this concept suggests that luck is when preparation meets opportunity. It's the intersection where hard work and chance converge, creating a moment ripe for success.

Preparation involves meticulous planning, learning, and rehearsing that one undertakes diligently. On the other hand, opportunity is the favorable juncture or set of circumstances that arise, often unexpectedly.

The roots of this idea stretch back to the ancient philosophers. Seneca, a Stoic philosopher, is often credited with asserting, "Luck is what happens when preparation meets opportunity." This timeless truth has traversed through centuries, finding relevance in various aspects of life and business.

In the broader scheme of things, this principle is not limited to individual moments of triumph but is a philosophy for life and career. It suggests that consistently preparing oneself for potential scenarios lays the groundwork for taking advantage of opportunities when they arise.

Consider the salesperson who spends hours researching a prospective client and understanding their needs, market position, and pain points. When an unexpected meeting with a key decision- maker occurs, they are ready to pitch their solution effectively. Or the entrepreneur who tirelessly refines their business model, and when a venture capitalist expresses interest, they are able to articulate their vision compellingly.

A common misconception is that preparation is a one-time event, a box to be checked before moving on. It's a continuous process of learning, practicing, and adapting. Now, let's dive deeper into the details.

Picture a tapestry of countless threads, each one representing an action, a decision, or a piece of knowledge gained. Preparation is like weaving these threads together daily, with patience and precision. It's the early mornings spent honing your pitch, the late nights spent studying market trends, and the relentless pursuit of personal and professional development.

Have you ever found yourself questioning the value of these efforts? Have you ever wondered if all this preparation is truly worth it?

Imagine this: you're in an elevator, and the CEO of a major company you've been trying to reach steps in. You only have a few floors to make an impression. Those hours of preparation, the elevator pitch you've rehearsed countless times, led to this moment. Your heart races, but the words flow effortlessly. This is not luck. This is a preparation meeting opportunity.

But how do we ensure that we are not just prepared but prepared in the right way? How do we anticipate the opportunities that might come our way?

First, we must understand our goals. What is it that we are striving for? Once we have clarity on our destination, we can begin to map out the path to get there. This involves setting objectives, learning new skills, and seeking knowledge that aligns with our ambitions.

Second, we must remain vigilant. Opportunities often come disguised as mundane interactions or chance encounters. The ability to see beyond the surface to recognize the potential in every situation sets the prepared mind apart.

Third, we must be adaptable. The landscape of business and life is ever-changing. What works today may not work tomorrow. Therefore, our preparation must be dynamic, evolving with the shifting tides of our environment.

And what about when things don't go as planned? When, despite all our preparation, does the opportunity slip through our fingers?

Herein lies another layer of preparation: resilience. Being prepared means gearing up for success and bracing for setbacks. It's about building the fortitude to face rejection, learn from it, and forge ahead.

Let me ask you, have you ever experienced a moment when all your preparation paid off in ways you never expected?

These are the stories that resonate and inspire us. They are the tales of individuals who were ready when their moment came, who seized it with both hands and turned it into something extraordinary.

Perhaps you're still waiting for that defining opportunity. Or maybe it's already come and gone, and you're wondering what's next. Remember that with every step you take, with every piece of knowledge you acquire, you are laying the foundation for future success.

In the pages to come, we will explore how to cultivate a mindset of preparation, sharpen our skills, and position ourselves to recognize and create opportunities. We will dissect the anatomy of preparation, looking at the habits, strategies, and attitudes that enable us to make the most of every opportunity.

And so, as we embark on this journey together, let us commit to the pursuit of preparation, not as a task, but as a way of life. For it is in these depths that we will unearth the treasures of our potential, setting the stage for a life where preparation meets opportunity and where opportunity ushers in the next level of selling—and the next level of life.

Strategic Networking for Sales Success

Strategic networking is a beacon for those seeking to elevate their sales game to unprecedented heights in a world of potential. It is a dance of connection, a symphony of relationships that, when orchestrated with skill and intention, opens doors to opportunities that might otherwise remain closed. Let us embark on a journey through the realm of strategic networking, where every handshake and every smile is a step towards the next level of selling—and life.

Our goal is to master the art of networking so that it becomes more than just an exchange of business cards—it becomes the catalyst for growth, innovation, and success. You will not only learn how to network, but you will understand the nuances of building relationships that are both meaningful and mutually beneficial.

Before we wade into the intricacies of networking, you must equip yourself with the necessary materials: a clear understanding of your business, a concise value proposition, a professional demeanor, an attentive ear, and an open mind. These are your tools; keep them sharpened and ready.

Now, let's paint a broad overview of the path ahead. We will begin by establishing your networking objectives and identifying and connecting with key individuals. Then, we will focus on nurturing these relationships, contributing value, and leveraging your network to open new sales opportunities.

Dive with me into the detailed steps. First, define what you wish to achieve through networking. Is it to find potential clients, partners, or mentors? With a defined purpose, your efforts will be focused and more effective. Next, research events, conferences, and social platforms where your desired contacts might gather. Prepare an engaging introduction that piques interest without sounding like a rehearsed sales pitch.

Imagine entering a room; the air is abuzz with conversation, potentially swirling around like an invisible force. Your goal is not to conquer this space but to become part of its rhythm. Begin with those who have no one to speak to them; the most profound connections are often made in the quiet corners.

Remember that listening is as important as speaking as you engage with others. Inquire about their work, their challenges, and their triumphs. Offer insights or assistance where you can, and when the time comes, share your own story with clarity and confidence.

Here's a practical tip: always follow up. A quick message or email after meeting someone can be the difference between a fleeting encounter and a lasting association. But beware: don't be too pushy or self-serving. Networking is a two-way street—it's about building trust and rapport over time.

How will you know if your networking efforts are successful? When new introductions lead to meaningful conversations, and when those conversations lead to opportunities for collaboration or sales, you are on the right track.

Do not be disheartened if you encounter difficulties, such as unresponsive contacts or a lack of leads. Troubleshoot by revisiting your approach—perhaps your pitch needs refining, or maybe you need to expand your horizons to new industries or events.

Now, imagine the ripple effect of a well-nurtured network. Picture the joy of unlocking a new level of professional potential, the exhilaration of a thriving sales career fueled by genuine relationships. This is not just about the immediate transaction; it's about planting seeds that will bear fruit in future seasons.

Have you ever considered the power of a single connection? One introduction could lead to a chain reaction of opportunities redefining your career. But it's up to you to initiate that first interaction, bridge the gap between stranger and collaborator, and transform a simple "hello" into a partnership that echoes through the annals of your professional journey.

As we close this chapter, remember that strategic networking is not a means to an end but a continuous endeavor. It's a commitment to growth, community, and the belief that we can achieve more together. Keep weaving your web of connections, for in this intricate pattern lies the key to next-level selling—and a next- level life.

The Power of Positivity

The power of positivity is not merely an abstract concept but a tangible force that molds our professional and personal lives. Like a beacon of light guiding ships through treacherous waters, a positive mindset illuminates the path to success, influencing outcomes and shaping destinies in the competitive realm of sales.

Picture a world where each morning greets you with a promise of new possibilities. The sun's rays penetrate the canopy of doubt, casting a glow on the day's prospects. This is the world you inhabit when you harness positivity. But what happens when negativity seeps into the crevices of your mind, casting a shadow over your ambitions?

Imagine encountering a sales professional, shoulders slumped, eyes downcast, voice tinged with defeat. This is someone who has succumbed to the weight of negative thinking, a mindset that sees challenges as insurmountable and failure as inevitable. The problem is not just an individual's flagging spirit; it's the pervasive impact on performance, morale, and the bottom line.

The consequences of neglecting the power of positivity can be dire. A sales team plagued by pessimism may be trapped in a cycle of missed targets and lost opportunities. Clients can sense desperation, which repels them, creating a self-fulfilling prophecy of failure. Negativity becomes a contagion, infecting all it touches and leaving a trail of unrealized potential in its wake.

So, what is the antidote to this malaise? The solution lies in cultivating a mindset of unwavering positivity. It's about seeing the glass not just half full but brimming with opportunities. The first step in this transformative journey is to acknowledge our thoughts' power and their influence over our reality.

To implement this solution, begin with self-awareness. Monitor your thoughts. When negativity whispers, counter it with affirmations of your skills and past successes. Surround yourself with positive influences—books, podcasts, colleagues who radiate optimism—and let their energy fuel your own.

Consider the story of a salesperson who decided to start each day with a clear vision of success. They visualized shaking hands on a deal, imagined the satisfaction of surpassing goals, and felt the elation of triumph in advance. This daily practice became a ritual, a mental rehearsal for success that, over time, translated into reality.

Evidence of the power of positivity is not just anecdotal; it's supported by research. Studies have shown that positive individuals often outperform their negative counterparts, not because they encounter fewer obstacles but because they perceive challenges as opportunities for growth. They rebound from setbacks more quickly and are more persistent in the face of rejection.

While some may argue that an optimistic outlook is simply one piece of the puzzle and that hard skills and strategy are equally important, the truth is that positivity amplifies the effectiveness of all other skills. It's the spark that ignites the engine of success.

Consider alternative solutions such as mindfulness or stress management techniques. These can complement the positive mindset by providing tools to maintain composure and clarity in high-pressure situations.

By now, you might be wondering how to maintain this positive outlook consistently. How do you fend off the creeping tendrils of doubt and negativity? It's simple yet challenging: choose to focus on the good, celebrate even the smallest victories, and treat failures as lessons rather than losses.

Envision yourself as a magnet, attracting success simply by virtue of your positive disposition. This is not a fanciful dream but a practical strategy. Positivity breeds confidence, and confidence is magnetic. It draws in prospects, encourages referrals, and opens doors to opportunities that might otherwise remain closed.

To conclude, the journey of sales is fraught with challenges, but the armor of positivity will protect you against the arrows of rejection and the swords of competition. Forge this armor with the steel of positive thoughts, the shield of a cheerful demeanor, and the sword of unwavering belief in your abilities. With this arsenal at your disposal, you are not just participating in the act of selling; you are embarking on a quest for next-level success in both sales and life.

Remember, the power of positivity is not just about feeling good; it's a strategic tool that can elevate your sales career to new heights. It's the difference between a life of mediocrity and a life of extraordinary achievements. So, as you turn the pages of this book and your life, ask yourself: Are you ready to embrace positivity and unlock the door to next-level selling—and a next-level life?

Recognizing and Seizing Sales Opportunities

The ability to discern and grasp sales opportunities as they arise is akin to a seasoned sailor navigating the capricious winds, steering towards the horizon of success. This skill, often overlooked, is a critical component of a sales professional's arsenal. It is the art of seeing beyond the immediate, of understanding the latent potential in a situation that may appear ordinary to an untrained eye. Let us embark on a journey to master this art, transforming how you engage with your sales environment and, consequently, your life.

To begin, consider the concept of opportunity recognition as a form of intuition sharpened by experience and knowledge. It is the capacity to identify a seed of potential in a conversation, a market change, or a client's strategy shift. Think of it as a sixth sense for business growth, where the indicators of opportunity are not always glaringly evident but are there, waiting to be uncovered by the astute observer.

Imagine walking into a room where potential clients discuss their challenges. Amongst the cacophony of voices, an adept salesperson hears problems, unvoiced needs, and unmet desires that whisper the chance to offer a solution. This is where the magic happens—where a problem becomes an opportunity, where a complaint transforms into a sale.

Now, let's dive into the practical side with an illustrative example. Picture Jane, a sales representative for a tech firm. During a routine follow-up call with a client, she notices a hint of frustration in the client's voice regarding their current software system's limitations. Instead of merely empathizing, Jane sees a door slightly ajar. She inquires further, gathers details, and recognizes an opportunity to offer a more advanced solution. This is the crux of the matter—opportunity recognition often requires active listening and probing beneath the surface.

From a different angle, consider the impact of market trends and how they create opportunities. A salesperson attuned to the ebbs and flows of their industry can anticipate needs before they become apparent to others. Take, for instance, the rise of remote work. A sales professional who recognizes this trend early on can pivot their offerings to include products or services that facilitate this new mode of operation, thus capturing a market segment that competitors have yet to notice.

Supporting our exploration with data, studies have indicated that high-performing salespeople possess a superior ability to identify opportunities. They exhibit a mindset that is constantly scanning the environment for cues and clues that signal a chance to add value for their clients and, by extension, for their own company.

When dealing with complex terms such as 'latent need identification' or 'market trend analysis,' it is crucial to break these down. Latent need identification is about uncovering needs that the client may not even be aware of, while market trend analysis involves examining the direction in which the market is moving to predict future needs.

As we draw this exploration close, let's summarize the key takeaways. Recognizing and seizing sales opportunities is about being perceptive, proactive, and knowledgeable. It's about listening for the unspoken, observing the unnoticed, and acting on the potential for growth.

Are you attuned to the subtle signals around you that could signify a chance to advance? Can you pivot and adapt when the winds of market change blow? Remember, the sales landscape is rich with hidden gems of opportunity, waiting to be unearthed by those with the vision to see them.

As you continue through this book and your journey in sales, consider this: every interaction, every market shift, and every piece of client feedback is a puzzle piece in the grand picture of opportunities. It is your task to assemble these pieces into a mosaic of success. Will you rise to the challenge and seize the sales opportunities that are waiting for you?

In the world of sales, as in life, it is often the small moments, the seemingly inconsequential decisions, that can lead to the most significant breakthroughs. Keep your senses sharp, your mind open, and your actions ready. The next level of selling—and the next level of life—is there for the taking for those who have the vision to recognize it and the courage to seize it.

Sales Success: Hard Work or Luck?

In the ever-evolving tapestry of sales, the threads of hard work and luck intertwine to create a narrative of success that is as varied as the salespeople who weave it. The question of whether hard work or luck plays the more pivotal role in sales success is one that has sparked debates among novices and veterans alike. It is a pertinent inquiry that begs for a deeper understanding of the forces at play in the high-stakes world of selling.

Why, one might wonder, should we embark on a comparative analysis of these two elements? The answer is that understanding the relative contributions of hard work and luck can significantly impact training, development, and motivation strategies within the sales profession. It also offers insights into how salespeople can best position themselves for success in an unpredictable market.

As we establish criteria for our comparison, let us consider the definitions and manifestations of hard work and luck in the domain of sales. Hard work encompasses the dedication, effort, and persistence applied consistently over time. It includes the relentless pursuit of knowledge, the refinement of sales techniques, and the strategic planning that goes into cultivating relationships and closing deals. Conversely, luck is often viewed as the serendipitous element—the chance encounters, the timing of market fluctuations, and the unforeseeable opportunities that fall into one's lap.

When we directly compare these subjects, we find that hard work and luck are common contributors to sales success. Both can lead to the right place at the right time scenario—hard work by strategically positioning oneself and luck by sheer coincidence. Both can also amplify the other; hard work can increase the probability of encountering lucky breaks, while luck can propel the results of hard work to new heights.

Yet, as we shift to direct contrast, the distinctions become clear. Hard work is within one's control; it results from deliberate actions and decisions. Luck, however, is inherently unpredictable and cannot be relied upon as a strategy. It's the wild card in the sales deck, capable of changing the game but elusive.

Visual aids such as graphs or charts could be employed to illustrate the frequency and impact of luck in sales success compared to the steady trajectory that hard work typically follows. However, the essence of this discussion is best captured through narrative and rich description, painting a picture of the salesperson's journey marked by both disciplined effort and fortuitous occurrences.

Diving deeper, our analysis reveals that hard work and luck are not mutually exclusive but are rather complementary forces. Hard work lays the groundwork for success, creating a fertile field where the seeds of luck may sprout. A salesperson's disciplined approach to prospecting, follow-up, and service creates multiple pathways for potential lucky breaks.

The contemporary relevance of this debate is seen in stories of overnight successes or sudden market shifts that create unexpected demand for a product or service. Yet, behind every 'overnight success' is often a backstory of relentless hard work and preparation that positioned the individual to capitalize on the moment when luck struck.

Are you not convinced that your tireless efforts will pay off, or do you perhaps secretly hope for that lucky break to catapult you to the top? Consider the story of Jonathan, a diligent sales consultant who spent years building his expertise and network. His 'big break' came when an industry leader unexpectedly attended one of his workshops. Was it luck that this influencer was in the audience, or was it the result of Jonathan's years of hard work in establishing a reputation that attracted such a clientele?

And so, as we ponder the roles of hard work and luck, it becomes evident that while luck can provide opportunities, it is often the hard work that prepares one to seize them. A stroke of luck might open a door, but the skill, honed by hard work, allows one to walk through it confidently.

To reach the next level of selling—and indeed, the next level of life—one must acknowledge the role of luck and embrace the certainty of hard work. In the fabric of your sales career, you will find that the most vibrant patterns are those where the threads of hard work are woven tightly together, ready to catch the glimmering strands of luck when they appear.

In conclusion, the journey to sales success is marked by the footprints of dedication and the occasional wings of fortune. As you turn the pages of this book and the chapters of your sales career, remember that the pursuit of excellence is a deliberate one, punctuated by moments of serendipity that can either be fleeting or transformative depending on how ready you are to receive them.

The Role of Intuition in Sales

Intuition often appears cloaked in mystery, an elusive whisper guiding us through life's labyrinth. It's a sensation most of us have encountered, whether deciding which path to take on a walk or which choice to make in a pivotal life moment. In the realm of sales, intuition can be just as influential, though it may not always be recognized for its powerful tool.

At its core, intuition is the ability to understand something instinctively without needing conscious reasoning. It's a gut feeling, a hunch, an internal compass that points us toward a direction that logic alone may not illuminate. To elaborate on its key elements, intuition is often described as the sum of our experiences, knowledge, and sensory inputs that our brain processes at a speed that outpaces our conscious thought, delivering an almost instantaneous verdict on the matter at hand.

While the concept of intuition is ancient, the term itself comes from the Latin 'intueri', which means 'to look inside' or 'to contemplate'. This etymological root captures the essence of intuition as a form of internal observation. To contextualize it within a broader framework, intuition acts as an undercurrent in the vast ocean of decision-making processes, subtly influencing the course of our actions with its silent sway.

In the context of sales, intuition manifests in various scenarios. A seasoned salesperson might walk into a room and immediately sense the mood, adjusting their pitch before a word is spoken. Another may inexplicably feel drawn to call a dormant lead, only to find that the timing is unexpectedly perfect. These 'lucky' opportunities are often the fruit of an intuitive nudge.

It's imperative to address some common misconceptions about intuition in sales. Far from being an esoteric force, intuition is a practical asset. It does not mean disregarding data or analytics; it involves synthesizing these with an inner sense of knowing to make more informed decisions. To illustrate, imagine a salesperson considering two prospects. On paper, both seem equally promising, but intuition might signal that one prospect has a slightly higher potential for conversion, perhaps due to subtle cues picked up during initial interactions.

But how does one cultivate this subtle art? Begin by listening.

Not just to the words of your clients but to the tone of their voice, the pace of their speech, and the unspoken messages their body language conveys. Reflect on your experiences, absorbing the patterns and lessons they weave into your professional tapestry.

Why should you trust this invisible guide? Consider the tale of a sales professional we'll call Sarah. Her data suggested that pursuing a particular client might not be worthwhile. Yet, something within her urged a different course of action. She followed that instinct and invested time in nurturing the relationship, and it blossomed into one of the most lucrative accounts of her career. Was it just a lucky guess, or was it Sarah's intuition discerning a diamond in the rough?

Perhaps you're skeptical of such narratives. You might ask, "Can intuition truly be a reliable ally in the cutthroat sales world?" To answer that, let's dive into the essence of what it means to sell. Sales are not merely about transactions; they're about connections, understanding needs, educating, and providing solutions. Every interaction, every success, and every setback hone your intuition. It is the silent partner to your conscious strategies, offering guidance that can lead to serendipitous victories.

Maintaining a balance to harness intuition's power fully is crucial. A strong foundation in the fundamentals of selling—knowledge of your product, market analysis, and strategic planning—should always be the bedrock upon which your sales approach is built. Intuition does not replace these elements; it complements them. The spark can ignite a deeper conversation, the insight that can reveal an unspoken objection or the timing to close a deal at just the right moment.

In the end, the role of intuition in sales is akin to the subtle art of sailing. You can master the mechanics, study the charts, and understand the weather patterns, but the feel of the wind on your face and the taste of the salt in the air guides you to unseen shores. As you navigate the waters of your sales career, allow intuition to be your silent sentinel, watching over the horizon for the 'lucky' opportunities that are waiting to be discovered.

Remember, the next level of selling isn't just about the numbers; it's about elevating every facet of your craft, including the intangible. Next level life? That's about trusting yourself to sail even when the map ends, knowing that your intuition has been charting the course all along.

CHAPTER 15

CONCLUSION

In this final chapter, we have embarked on a transformative journey through the world of consultative selling and the art of building genuine connections. We have explored the mindset, strategies, and techniques that set-top salespeople apart and enable them to create personalized and compelling sales experiences. Now, as we reach the end of our exploration, it is time to reflect on the key points and lessons learned throughout the chapters and provide a final message of encouragement and inspiration.

Throughout the book, I have emphasized the importance of embracing the consultant within and prioritizing the customer's needs. We have seen how building trust and genuine connections can lead to long-term success in sales, far beyond the traditional focus on pushing products. By adopting a consultative approach, you have the power to transform prospects into loyal customers eager to do business with you.

The selling discipline has been a recurring theme, reminding us of the importance of daily routines and long-term strategies. We have explored the art of story selling, understanding the impact of belief systems and sales behaviors, and mastering the art of consultative closing. Each topic has provided valuable insights and practical techniques to enhance your sales performance.

We have deconstructed the sales process, ensuring that you have a clear path to follow for consistent results. From tactical sales planning to follow-up mastery, we have covered the essential components of sales success. We have also delved into the often-overlooked connection between physical health, mental well-being, and sales performance, highlighting the importance of taking care of yourself to excel in your sales career.

As we conclude, it is essential to remember that external factors do not solely determine success in sales. Your mindset, beliefs, and actions also influence it. By cultivating a sales mindset focused on continuous improvement, embracing challenges, and leveraging your strengths, you have the power to overcome obstacles and achieve remarkable results.

I want to commend you for taking the time to invest in your growth as a salesperson. You have taken a significant step towards reaching your full potential by reading this book and implementing the strategies and techniques shared within its pages. Remember that success in sales is not an endpoint but a continuous journey of learning, adapting, and evolving.

I want to leave you with this final message: You have the power to elevate your sales career to the next level. Embrace the consultative approach, build genuine connections, and always prioritize your customers' needs. Believe in yourself and your ability to succeed, and never stop striving for excellence. With dedication, perseverance, and a commitment to continuous improvement, you CAN achieve extraordinary results in your sales journey.

Thank you for joining me on this transformative exploration of next-level selling, leading you to a next-level life. May this book serve as a guide and a source of inspiration as you navigate the exciting and lucrative world of consultative selling. Remember, the greatest close a salesperson can have is when the prospect says, "Let's do this!" Now... Go out and MAKE IT A GREAT DAY!

To contact Michael Paulk about speaking, coaching, or training opportunities, visit his website: www.MichaelPaulk.com and click on the contact tab.

www.ingramcontent.com/pod-product-compliance
Lightning Source LLC
Chambersburg PA
CBHW071030290526
45795CB00004B/1170